Also by Philip Katcher:

*Encyclopedia of British, Provincial and German Units*
*American Provincial Corps*
*The American War 1812–14*
*The Army of the Potomac*
*The Army of Northern Virginia*

# Philip Katcher

# ARMIES OF THE AMERICAN WARS
# 1753–1815

clw8

HASTINGS HOUSE, PUBLISHERS
New York

Library of Congress Cataloging in publication data.
Katcher, Philip R. N.
    Armies of the American Wars, 1753–1815.

    Bibliography: p. 153
    Includes index.
    1. Armies – History. 2. North America – History,
Military. I. Title.
UA15.K36     355'.0097     75–9602
ISBN 0–8038–0389–3
First published in the United States 1975 by HASTINGS
HOUSE, PUBLISHERS, INC.

*Printed in Great Britain*

*to Rebecca*

# Contents

# Illustrations

*Author's Acknowledgement*

Thanks are due for all their help to René
Chartbrand of Canada; Richard Claydon,
Colonel William Perryman, and Timothy Terrell
of the United States; and G. A. Embleton of
Great Britain. Special thanks are due to my wife
for her great help in all phases of writing this
book.

# 1

# The French Army in America

There is a particularly fresh and alive feeling on a May morning, just after a rainfall, in those dense, virgin woods which made up America in 1754. The leaves seem a vivid, neon green, almost translucent. The woods are alive with small spring sounds. Water drips slowly, suddenly in heavy splashes, from the leaves. A few birds sing, but not many find their way into such dense woods. The squirrels, chipmunks and foxes out for their breakfasts make almost no noise at all.

On this particular May morning, in these particular woods in territory disputed between Briton and Frenchman, there are other sounds. Campfires crackle, pots of steaming soup simmer, and the melodic sound of the French language joins the wildlife sounds. It is a party under the command of a regular French officer, Ensign Joseph Coulon de Villiers, the Sieur de Jumonville. The men have camped in a rocky glen, at the bottom of a valley. While they cook their breakfasts, their muskets lean beneath a nearby ledge, put there the previous night to keep them dry in the night's rainstorm.

There is, however, yet another sound, as unheard by the Frenchmen as the sounds of the chipmunks. It is the sound of men of the Virginia Regiment, and some Indian allies, under the command of Lieutenant-Colonel George Washington, who are even now surrounding the French camp. It had been reported to the British colonists by an Irish interpreter that the French were headed east, 'resolved to strike the first English they meet'. Washington has determined to strike them first instead.

Now, at seven o'clock, the sun has just risen. At a sudden signal from Washington, the British jump to their feet and open fire. There is a startled pause

among the French; then they, too, jump to their feet and scramble for their muskets. For about fifteen minutes both sides exchange fire, but, heavily outnumbered, the French begin throwing down their arms. With that the Indians run into the camp, scalping both dead and wounded. A British eyewitness reported that the Indian leader, the Half King, challenged Jumonville after the firing was over, and, in the following fight, split open his skull and washed his hands in his brains.

It was a harsh beginning to what would be a harsh and long war. Debates went on and on about what the French were actually doing in those woods that May morning. The British claimed it was a raiding party, the French that it was a diplomatic party sent to warn the British away from French territory. Neither side really expected, or wanted, this to start a full-fledged war, and officially war wasn't declared for two more years, but real fighting was now underway.

The French were not really prepared for a major war in America. In 1665 King Louis XIV sent a regular regiment, the Carignan Salières, to fight Indians, but the regiment had been disbanded a few years later. Defence had been left to the Canadian militia, which had been organized by Canada's Governor Frontenac in 1672.

Under the system he devised, each parish had to provide a company, with a quota system built into each company so that a proportion of men would always stay behind to work the farms and small industries necessary to support the colony. Every able-bodied man between the ages of fifteen and sixty was eligible, and theoretically during the Seven Years War some 15,000 men were available for service. Actually, in 1758 only 1,100 were called up, and another 4,000 were used to transport and supply the fighting forces.

Militiamen were not paid, but they did receive a musket, bayonet, and ammunition. Furthermore, they could buy their musket at an artificially low cost and keep it after being demobilized, which was a major inducement in getting men to join.

There were no militia uniforms. Each man wore his own civilian clothing, often a mixture of French

*The white tunque marks this man as being a member of the Trois Rivières Militia. Otherwise, his dress is typically civilian. He has been issued with a musket and powder-flask and carries his bullets in a pouch on his waistbelt. (Roffe/Osprey)*

civilian, frontier buckskins, and Indian garb. In fact, many of them were little better than Indians, taking scalps and living Indian-style lives. This type of trooper made an excellent scout, and performed magnificently on raiding parties but, when facing regular troops in a European-style pitched battle, was apt to break and run on the first volley.

The militia was, regardless of its virtues, necessary in the planning of Canada's defence. In 1759 the companies were gathered into three regional brigades. Each man was issued a knitted tunque (a sort of stocking-cap) of a different colour according to his brigade. Men from Quebec wore red, men from Trois Rivières white, and those from Montreal blue. That was as uniform as the men ever became.

Another, even less disciplined force, was made up of the *courers de bois* – backwoodsmen, trappers, and foresters. Virtually outcasts from the formal, almost feudal society of New France, they knew the forests and its ins and outs like no other Europeans. Although of minimal value in any formal campaign, their war-parties struck fear into the heart of every British colonist and caused many British troops to be tied up in local defence.

The avenging raiding party would consist of Indians, several *courers de bois*, some militiamen and colonial troops, and a partisan leader such as the bold and resourceful Marin or Langade. At times

*Contemporary sketches of Indians in their wild, free state, showing, 'an Indian pursuing a wounded enemy with his Tomahawk' and 'an Indian dress'd for War, with a Scalp'. (Courtauld Institute)*

some young French regular officers, often painted as Indians, would come along for the experience. The parties would make their ways through the woods and fall on some small settlement or a single farmer digging out a meagre living on a small plot on the frontier. The result would usually be scalpings, rapings – although not by the Indians, who thought such activities sapped them of strength – and cannibalism.

Indians served well on such parties, and their fighting at Braddock's defeat was excellent in all ways. But that was about as much as they really contributed to the French cause. They tended to need to give and to hear constant, long, and tedious speeches of how magnificent a fighting group they were, at the same time appearing and disappearing at their own whim. They constantly demanded hatchets, guns, liquor, and everything else the Europeans had.

Louis-Joseph, Marquis de Montcalm-Gozon de Saint Véran, commander of His Christian Majesty's troops in Canada, wrote to his wife that the Indians were an impossible lot. 'One needs the patience of an angel to get on with them. Ever since I have been here, I have had nothing but visits, harangues, and deputations of these gentry. . . . They make war with astounding cruelty, sparing neither men, women nor children.'

It was actually the 'Christian' Indians, Indians who lived on the Jesuit missions, who were the most unreliable. They came largely from the Hurons of Lorette, the Abenakis of St Francis and Batiscan, the Iroquois of Caughnawaga and La Présentation, and the Iroquois and Algonquins of the Two Mountains on the Ottawa. Constant exposure to European 'civilization' had sapped their fighting

*This* coureur de bois *has been to the far western reaches of New France. His dress is typical of western plains Indians whom he probably met along the Mississippi.* (Roffe/Osprey)

abilities, while making them dependent on what only Europeans could supply – mostly drink.

Indians tended to be perhaps not so much dressed as undressed. 'I see no difference', wrote Montcalm's aide, Bougainville, 'in the dress, ornaments, dances, and songs of the various western (Indian) nations. They go naked, excepting a strip of cloth passed through a belt.' A missionary went further with the description.

'Imagine a great assembly of savages adorned with every ornament most suited to disfigure them in European eyes, painted with vermilion, white, green, yellow, and black . . . methodically laid on with the help of a little tallow, which serves for pomatum. The head is shaved except at the top, where there is a small tuft, to which are fastened feathers, a few beads of wampum, or some such trinket. . . . Pendants hang from the nose, and also from the ears, which are split in infancy and drawn with weights till they flap at last against the shoulders!'

Regardless of how they may have looked, or how the French may have personally felt about them, it was true, as Bougainville wrote, that 'here in the forests of America we can no more do without them than cavalry on the plains'.

Obviously this motley collection of Indians, local farmers, and wild backwoodsmen could not defend Canada against regulars in a real war. Since the colonies were governed by the Department of Marine Affairs, it was this department that, about 1680, organized the first permanent troops to garrison its posts. They were Les Compagnies Franches de la Marine, the Independent Companies of Marines. Not on any army lists, they were organized in bodies no larger than a company. A naval lieutenant became a Marine captain, commanding a company. The rest of his company was made up of a lieutenant, an ensign, two sergeants, four corporals, a drummer, and a fifer. The number of privates varied, reaching a low of about thirty-five and a high of eighty.

It was these troops who were largely responsible for defending all of France's colonies. By 1755 there were 150 independent Marine companies in service, with thirty in Canada, although by 1757 there were forty in Canada. Another thirty-six companies were in Louisiana, twenty-four garrisoned the great stone fortress of Louisbourg, in what is now Nova Scotia. There were twenty companies on the Windward Islands, another ten at Guyana, and thirty-two at Saint-Domingue.

There were actually foot soldiers, infantrymen, who were not shipboard marines in any way. The men themselves were Frenchmen, who, after their terms of service, were greatly encouraged to settle in the colonies in which they had served. As the war went on, and recruiting and reinforcing the companies grew more difficult, local men were accepted for service. Officers, on the other hand, were almost always drawn from the local population. They were members of the local *noblesse*, and were usually enlisted as *cadets à l'equillette* into a cadet corps established for the companies stationed in Canada, Louisbourg, and Louisiana. In 1730, the same year as the colonial cadet corps was set up, a similar corps was established at Rochefort, France, for the West Indies companies.

Each enlisted Marine was issued with a full set of clothing every two years, while every other year he received a new hat, waistcoat, breeches, two *roussi* shirts, stockings, a stock, and a pair of shoes. Furthermore, in Canada, each man received an overcoat, a blanket, a woollen cap, a pair of *mitasses* or leggings, two pairs of drawers, two hanks of thread and six needles, an awl, a tinderbox, a butcher's knife, a comb, and a tomahawk. He also received two knives called 'Siamese knives', a pair of mittens, two pairs of deerskin shoes, a dressed deerskin, two portage collars, and a drag-rope.

The uniforms themselves came from France, items being sent from various parts of the country to the seaports where they were made into full uniforms and shipped out. The coats were the standard infantryman's *justaucorps*, or regimental coat, made of heavy, coarse greyish-white wool with cuffs and linings made of an only slightly lighter-weight dark blue wool. The original marines of about 1700 had pewter buttons, but these were soon changed to brass.

Blue wool was also used for the waistcoat and breeches. Stockings were also blue. A black tricorne hat, bound up with a yellow 'false gold' woollen tape was worn. Stocks were white. Gaiters, which reached halfway up the thigh, were made of white duck and had some 20–24 buttons. Black shoes and a spare pair of soles were also issued.

Corporals wore the same uniform, with a yellow wool strip sewn round their cuffs. Sergeants had similar uniforms, but of better quality with a truer white cloth used for their coats. Their buttons were gilt and the hats were bound in fine gold. An inch-wide fine gold lace border worn around each cuff marked the wearer as a sergeant, while sergeant-majors had two gold lace stripes, as well as two more around each pocket flap.

Sergeants carried gold-hilted swords in gilt-tipped scabbards. Grenadier company sergeants had been allowed to arm themselves with muskets and bayonets as early as 1703, but the rest of the regimental sergeants carried halberds. The typical French halberd had a central spear-point with symmetrical lateral branches at the point's base. They were six feet, nine inches long, 'because two halberds are 13 half feet, which is the distance which must exist between each rank when they are formed for battle'.

Actually, halberds were highly unpopular weapons, and sergeants asked to be allowed to carry muskets and bayonets instead. In the colonies they probably did so before they did in France itself, but on 1 October 1758 halberds were ordered to be abandoned throughout the Army.

Much the same thing happened to the spontoons carried by officers. They were pole-arms between seven feet three inches and eight feet long, and on 1 December 1710 they had been ordered to be carried by colonels, lieutenant-colonels, and captains. Other officers were to carry muskets. In 1758, too, spontoons were ordered to be abandoned.

Also, like the sergeants, officers wore uniforms the same as their men, but of better quality. In 1731 Canadian officers requested that their uniforms be issued to them and from 1732 onwards this was the case. Officers, too, had gold buttons and hat-lace. Although they did not lace their coats, their waistcoats were often heavily laced in gold, depending on the owner's whim. Their main badge of rank was a gilt gorget, with a silver emblem, either the royal coat of arms or the anchor symbol of the Naval Department, worn on its centre.

Each company's drummer wore a blue coat, with red cuffs and lining, which was decorated profusely with the 'small' royal livery lace, a white chain on a crimson ground. The drum-major's lace was the 'great' livery lace, which was the same but with a silver stripe between the livery lace stripes. Their waistcoats, breeches, and stockings were of red wool, and their buttons were brass.

Drummers carried drums on buff belts with livery lace borders. The drums themselves were painted blue, at least according to one shipment to Louisbourg in 1744, and sprinkled with fleurs-de-lis, probably yellow. Drummers were also issued with brass-hilted swords, which they wore on buff leather belts trimmed with the livery lace.

Private soldiers' accoutrements consisted of a sword, brass-hilted and rather like an officer's sword, with two finger-holes made in the grip. As early as 1705 there had been complaints about the uselessness of these swords, and they were not often worn in Canada. On 20 March 1764 they were ordered to be officially abandoned for all men except sergeants, musicians, and grenadiers. Swords were carried in the same buff leather belts which held the iron triangular bayonets. Scabbards for both weapons were brass tipped. The belt itself had a brass frame buckle and was officially worn around the waist, over the coat. In America most men wore their belts slung over their right shoulders to their left hips, and this soon became regulation.

Plain wooden waterbottles, made like small, wood-bound kegs and probably locally procured, were used. Knapsacks were made of heavy duck, with a leather strap, and slung over the right shoulder.

The cartridge-box was also worn on a buff leather sling from the left shoulder to the right hip. The box itself was of reddish-brown leather, with the royal coat of arms impressed into its flap. A white leather anchor and border was usually sewn on to the flap of those boxes for Marines. Although appearing fairly large, the boxes held only between nine and twenty-seven rounds of ammunition. Soldiers also carried a number of different types of powder-horns.

Ammunition carried in the cartridge-boxes was used in a variety of muskets. The first model French musket was specified on 4 January 1717, and inspectors of the Royal Artillery Corps made sure that the Royal Manufactories at St Etienne, Maubeuge, and Nozon, near Charleville, kept strictly to the specifications. The musket chosen to be copied had a forty-six-inch barrel, with a bayonet-stud at its muzzle, and was fastened to the

*One of the finest military minds in an army rich with fine military minds – Louis-Joseph, Marquis de Montcalm-Gozon de Saint Véran.*

Pattern 1754 and 1763 muskets were also issued, but they had few changes from previous models.

The French issue musket was a good one – probably the best overall issued by any country of the period – but all flintlock muskets were, by modern standards, slow and cumbersome to load and fire. According to the *Drill of the French Infantry, Ordered by the King, 6 May, 1755*, quite a number of steps were required in its handling. The soldier held the

walnut stock with four pins. There was also a single band around the stock and barrel at the middle of the barrel, with a sling swivel set on the band's left side. Another sling swivel was attached to the stock just behind the screw plate. The 0·69-calibre musket was made with entirely iron furniture.

In 1728 another musket style was specified. It was similar in overall appearance to the 1717 model, but with three bands holding the barrel and stock together instead of the pins. This was a great improvement, because it made the barrel much easier to slip in and out of the stock for cleaning – without any danger of losing the old small pins. Another pattern musket, specified in 1746, replaced the old wooden ramrod with an iron one.

The wooden ramrod's replacement was a major step forward. The wooden one was easy to break in battle, and without a ramrod the musket was little better than a club. In addition, wood swelled in the damp and often the old ramrod was hard to get out of its channel under the barrel.

*'Christian' Indians were as interested in drinking and looting as fighting. This one has acquired a British waterbottle and gorget, and a European coat, which was especially favoured. Indians were, at best, undependable allies.* (Roffe/Osprey)

musket parallel with the ground, muzzle towards the enemy, with the lock close to his body and just above his waistbelt. In the wilderness each man would prime, load, and even fire, from this basic position pretty much according to his own will. In a formal, European-style battle, such as that of Quebec, firing, priming, and loading was done strictly by command.

The sergeant would call out, 'Half cock', then, 'Take out cartridge'. The soldier would half cock his musket, then reach round, open his cartridge-box flap and, without looking round, feel about until he touched a paper-wrapped cartridge containing ball and powder.

'Tear cartridge.' He would bring the cartridge up to his mouth and tear it open with his teeth – the real reason why recruits were required to have good teeth – exposing the black grains of powder

*Soldiers of the Compagnies Franches de la Marine spent most of their peaceful days in farming the land of some local seigneur. This one carries his water in a homemade plugged gourd. His clothing is his issue uniform, without the coat.* (Roffe/Osprey)

*In the winter, men of the Marine companies wore knitted tunque caps and blanket coats. Indian moccasins and garters were often popular, and men carried snowshoes and ice-creepers to make travel easier in the snowy wilderness. Beards were also warmer than clean-shaven faces.* (Roffe/Osprey)

butt down by his left foot, the muzzle now pointing in the air.

When the sergeant saw everyone was in that position, he would order, '*Mettez la cartouche dans le cannon*' (Place the cartridge in the barrel), whereupon the soldier would pour the powder down the barrel and drop the lead ball and brown paper after it. He then grabbed the ramrod's head and waited for the command, 'Withdraw the ramrod', followed by, 'Ram', and 'Replace the ramrod'. The powder was now nicely tamped down under the ball and paper. The weapon was primed, loaded, and ready to be fired. The soldier was then ordered to shoulder his arms, from which position he could fire, or march to another position, or be dismissed, as needed.

Firing was done quickly, with the commands, 'Ready your arms', 'Aim', and, 'Fire', following

*In the winter, soldiers wore locally made blanket coats called 'capotes', and mittens. The musket lock is wrapped to prevent the frizzen from getting damp, which is a sure cause of misfires. (G. A. Embleton, courtesy Tradition)*

within. Often some would spill on to his lips, leaving a terrible sulphur taste in his mouth.

'Prime'. He would look down and fill the iron pan of his musket with powder, making sure the small touch-hole was well covered. He then brought his hand to the frizzen, or battery, and, on the command, 'Close pan', snapped it tightly over the pan. 'Place the musket on the side of the sword', came the next order, although the French, '*Passez vos armes du côté de l'épée*', has a much finer ring to it than the English. On this command the soldier moved slightly facing front, dropping his musket

*Sergeant's lace in the Royal Roussillon was worn as on cuff A. The other lace patterns are those of a corporal in the Béarn (B), La Sarre (C), and Guyenne (D). (G. A. Embleton, courtesy Tradition)*

A regimental colonel carried a
spontoon, as well as having a
magnificently embroidered coat and
waistcoat. This illustration was
drawn by Colonel S. R. Baudouin,
French Guards Regiment, to
accompany the official drill manual
of 1755.

The lieutenant and ensign were to
carry fusils and cartridge-boxes.

rapidly on each other. If he were lucky, his weapon would discharge smoothly and fairly rapidly. There was, however, a lag between pulling the trigger and having the whole weapon go off, that one could almost time. Quite often, too, the weapon would fail to spark, or the pan alone would go off because of some object blocking the touch-hole, and the soldier would have to reprime and try again.

It sounds like a slow and cumbersome process, compared to modern self-priming cartridges used

*This officer of the Régiment de Languedoc has put aside his coat and wears his laced veste for summer campaigning. His campaign leggings are made of leather and he wears the highly popular plush breeches. His weapon is a beautifully made fusil.* (Roffe/Osprey)

*The sergeant's halberd, carried by a sergeant of le Régiment de Royal Roussillon, was highly unpopular, and replaced by a musket on most campaigns. The practice of wearing the sword-belt over the shoulder was also popular for campaigns.* (Roffe/Osprey)

in semi-automatic weapons, and it was. It worked, however, and faster than one might think. Any well-trained soldier was able to get off slightly more than three rounds a minute. The British, of course, had weapons which worked identically, and, in fact, virtually all European and American firearms worked identically until the invention of the percussion cap in 1815. Drill manuals designed for using such weapons were also quite similar in all armies of the times.

*This captain, commanding a company in the Régiment de Berry, is marked by his spontoon, as well as his gorget. His* veste *is laced gold and his stock is white although a common soldier's black stock was sometimes worn in the field.* (Roffe/Osprey)

*In 1757, twenty officers and men of the Corps Royal d'Artillerie were sent to help work the guns of Louisbourg. Among their ranks were men like this* cadet-gentilhomme, *who were sent to learn the martial arts in the field. They were under the direction of non-commissioned officers but did not have to perform fatigue duties. They were distinguished from common soldiers by their shoulder-knots, although the rest of the uniform was the same.* (Roffe/Osprey)

*Standard French accoutrements. The plain leather boxes are those of fusiliers, while the large one with the royal coat of arms impressed into its flap is for grenadiers. A powder-flask hangs below. The fusilier's sword and bayonet are shown in the waistbelt, while the other sword is the grenadier's issue.*

There were larger firearms than muskets on the battlefields – cannon. An artillery company, the Canonniers-Bombardiers, was raised to man the guns at Louisbourg, and proved such a success it was followed by two more companies of Canonniers-Bombardiers being raised in Saint-Domingue in 1745, the Windward Islands in 1747, Canada in 1750, and Louisiana in 1759. By 1762 only the two Saint-Domingue companies remained, joined by the survivors of all the other companies, and even they were drafted into the army's Royal Artillery Corps in 1766.

Cannoneers of the Canonniers-Bombardiers received heavy blue wool coats, with red wool cuffs and linings. Their waistcoats, breeches, and stockings were also red, and pewter buttons were worn on waistcoats and breeches. Their black tricorne hats were bound in white, or 'false silver', tape. The rest of their uniform was the same as the Marine companies.

Corporals had the same uniform, but with true scarlet cuffs instead of the dirty-looking, brick-coloured red wool used on privates' coats. Their buttons were silver-plated, and their hat lace was made with real silver. A strip of silver lace was sewn round each cuff. Sergeants had the same uniform, but with two silver lace strips on each cuff. Sergeants' swords were also silver-plated, as were their scabbard-tips, and their sword-knots were a mixture of red, blue, and silver.

Officer's uniforms were of even better quality, with silver buttons bearing a rosette in the centre and a thin border around the rim. They wore hats of 'half-beaver' bound with silver. All French officers had designs embroidered in facing colour thread where their coat-skirts were hooked back.

Drummers wore an identical uniform, only with the royal 'small' livery lace. Their hangers, or

*According to the 1755 French drill manual, regiments were to fire in three ranks, first rank kneeling. Here they take aim, which will quickly be followed by the command, 'Fire!'*

12

short swords, were the same as the cannoneers. All ranks were issued with blue surtouts, each with a dozen pewter buttons, to wear for fatigue. The drummer's surtout was marked with the 'small' livery lace as well. It was this surtout, or simply a waistcoat and shirtsleeves, which the men wore when in action. Only the officer in command of the piece remained fully uniformed and accoutred.

Men of the Canonniers-Bombardiers, like the men of the Compagnies Franches de la Marine, were colonial troops and their regimental coats were made without collars. It was not until September 1759 that colonial troops were allowed to wear collars. Another difference between them and Regular Army troops was that they carried naval muskets, made like the 1728 Army pattern, only with pins instead of bands used to keep the barrel

and stock together. Actually, all their arms were of poor quality, one officer noting in 1755 that, 'The refuse arms of all the king's arsenals had been sent to this country. It was the same with the artillery, the cannon being all damaged by rust.'

Not only were they not as well equipped as Regular Army troops, they did not even all get the uniforms they were supposed to. Out west, in Michilimackinac, now in Michigan, United States, for example, it was too difficult and expensive to ship replacement clothing and accoutrements

*When men went into camp or halted, they would ground their muskets facing the enemy in line of battle, before they began their fatigue duties. If suddenly attacked, they could quickly return to their muskets, ready for action. Note how the soldier holds his cartridge-box sling to keep it from flopping about.*

through the wilderness, and the men were clad in odd civilian and Indian clothes. An officer at the battle of Monongahela in 1755 had only his gorget, worn over his buckskins, to show he was, in fact, an officer. In Louisiana the Marines replaced their bayonets with tomahawks.

It was obvious that when a major war broke out and regular British regiments were sent to America, regular French regiments would have to go as well. It had been done before. In 1745 the great fortress of

Louisbourg had had a garrison of 560 troops, of which eight companies were from Les Compagnies Franches de la Marine, and two were from the Régiment Karrer.

The latter was a regiment of Swiss mercenaries, the only one recruited for service in the colonies. They were good men, able fighters as the siege in 1745 proved, but the harsh living conditions, long arrears in pay, and scant rations caused them, as well as the Marines, to mutiny. After the fortress

*An essential way of distinguishing regiments, as well as facing and* veste *colours, was the shape and number of buttons on the coat pockets. This fusilier of the Régiment de Béarn wears his unit's full uniform with its unique pockets.* (Roffe/Osprey)

*French military engineers were probably the best and most professional in the world at this time. Their uniform featured black plush velvet cuffs and gilt buttons arranged in fives. The rest of the uniform is that of a typical officer.* (Roffe/Osprey)

fell to the New England militia force, and the men were returned to France, the ringleaders were executed. No more Swiss were sent to America.

Instead, in 1755, the government decided to send six regular French battalions. These were taken from the Régiments de La Reine, Artois, Guyenne, Languedoc, Béarn, and Bourgogne, and sent under the command of Baron Dieskau. Only a year later, as conditions worsened, the government sent over Montcalm, accompanied by two battalions of La Sarre and the Royal Roussillon. The typical French regiment was made up of two battalions.

*Major-General le Marquis de Montcalm wears a fully embroidered coat and waistcoat, with the armour as worn by important generals as much as a badge of rank as for safety. This regulation uniform was worn by generals only when on campaign. It was this uniform Montcalm was wearing when mortally wounded at Quebec. (Roffe/Osprey)*

15

*The three regiments sent to garrison Louisbourg in 1758 were Bourgogne, Artois, and Cambis. The* justaucorps, *or regimental coats, of these were as shown above, with all-white coats for the first two and red collars and cuffs for the second.* (G. A. Embleton)

This group of some 3,800 men was the main line of French defence. The battalions of Artois, Bourgogne, and Cambis were sent to garrison Louisbourg where they (as had the previous garrison) fell under siege and eventually surrendered.

Some Regular Army Royal Artillerymen and Royal Engineers accompanied Montcalm's party, in addition to infantry.

On the way over, a ship of the British Royal Navy captured a French ship with four companies of Régiments Languedoc and La Reine, and these companies were not replaced until late 1757, so those two battalions were the smallest of the force. Otherwise, each battalion was to muster about 500 men, divided into one grenadier, one 'piquet' or light, and eight fusilier companies. The piquet company concept was a relatively new one, adopted when it was seen how lightly armed troops could work so much better in woods than could regular ones.

Each company was to be made up of a captain, a lieutenant, an ensign, several cadets, two sergeants and two corporals, a drummer, and some forty-five men. Beside the company officers, each battalion had a lieutenant-colonel and an adjutant. There was no rank of major, the senior captain assuming command after the lieutenant-colonel's loss and, indeed, the usual way of promotion was directly from captain to lieutenant-colonel.

In America the battalions fell under strength, and replacements were hard to obtain. A British officer, held prisoner in Quebec in 1755, made the following observations:

'I judge the whole militia of the country from 15 to 60 all of whom are ordered out to be about 25,000 – the regulars
    1 Battalion of the Régiment La Reine
    1 Battalion of the Régiment De Guinne
    1 Battalion of the Régiment Languedoc
    1 Battalion of the Régiment Bearre or some such
      name
    1 Battalion of the Régiment La Saar
    1 Battalion of the Régiment Royal Roussillon
    2 Battalions of the Régiment Berry

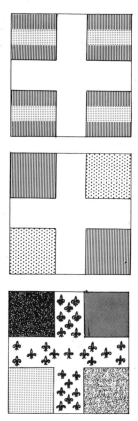

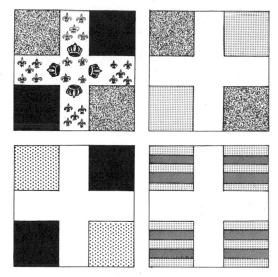

*Top, the colours of the Régiment de La Reine, left, which is quartered first and third green, second and fourth black. A white cross bears gold fleurs-de-lis, and gold and red crowns. Right, that of de Guyenne, quartered first and third green, second and fourth pale buff, with a white cross. Bottom left, La Sarre which has its first and third quarters dark reddish brown, other two black, and a white cross. Right, Béarn, with two scarlet and three pale buff stripes in each quarter, with a white cross.* (R. G. Windrow)

*Top, the colour of the Régiment de Berry, with two violet and one pale buff stripe in each quarter with a white cross. Middle, that of Languedoc, which has its first and third quarters in violet, while the other two are dark brown. The cross is white. Bottom, the colour of the Royal Roussillon, which has quarters of dark blue, scarlet, green, and pale buff, and gold fleurs-de-lis scattered on its white cross.* (R. G. Windrow)

Eight battalions which I don't think are much
    above half compleat.

'Thirty-six companies of the troupes de Maris (Marines) of the establishment 70 men each tho' at present not compleat. There were originally of these only twenty-six companies of forty men there was afterwards an addition of ten companies and the whole augmented to seventy men a company.

'It was reported amongst the vulgar that ten thousand men were expected out this spring but the officers did not expect above four or five battalions at most.'

The regular regiments were uniformed, equipped, and armed much as the colonial ones. Actually, according to the French colonial archives, the regiments left their old uniforms in France, upon being shipped to Canada, and received new ones. Their muskets were usually the latest patterns, and their kit of better quality and less mixed with locally produced items. Their regulation *justaucorps* were made with collars, save those of two of the three regiments which were to garrison Louisbourg. The Régiment Bourgogne had no collar and an all-white coat, as did that of Artois. The latter regiment was raised in 1673 as Régiment la Saint-Vallier.

The final regiment at Louisbourg was Cambis, which wore red collars, cuffs, and waistcoats. Régiment Cambis had been created as Régiment Vivonne in 1676 and had gone through a number of name changes by this time. Some men of the Volon-

*On the march, men carried their food and spare clothing in a* de la Parterie *knapsack. This corporal of the Régiment de Guyenne also carries his tent poles and an iron pot to cook rations to be shared by four men.* (Roffe/Osprey)

*An officer of Languedoc wrote that they had 'nothing but pease and bacon on the mess-table. Luckily the lakes are full of fish and both officers and soldiers have to turn fishermen.' This corporal of the Régiment de La Sarre has had a successful fishing expedition.* (Roffe/Osprey)

taires Etrangers also served in the Louisbourg garrison.

Other regiments, besides those at Louisbourg, were also old, well-established ones. Régiment de La Reine had been formed as six companies of the Régiment de Limosin as early as 1635. Its collar and cuffs were red, but its waistcoats were blue, and each coat pocket had eight pewter buttons, arranged with four on each side, while each sleeve had three buttons. The hats were bound in white or silver.

Régiment la Sarre had been created as the Régiment la Ferté-Sennecterre, and received its present name in 1685. Its collar and cuffs were blue, with red waistcoats, and three brass buttons on each pocket flap and cuff.

The Régiment Royal Roussillon was an especially old and fine one. It had been raised by Cardinal Mazarin about 1657 from the areas of Roussillon

*This grenadier of the Régiment de Cambis engages in one of the soldier's favourite pastimes, gambling. His open* veste *shows the white linen, collarless shirt, made pullover fashion. He wears a belt around his waist, but breeches are made to fit tightly and adjust by means of strings in the back so, actually, no belt was called for.* (Roffe/Osprey)

*In the summer the* justaucorps *was often discarded in favour of the regimental sleeved* veste. *Swords, too, were often laid aside. This fusilier of the Régiment de La Reine has lost his cockade and replaced it with feathers – a common practice in the wilderness.* (Roffe/Osprey)

and Catalonia, with the title of Catalan-Mazarin. In 1667 it was taken on the Royal Establishment, with its new name assigned. The regiment, as all Royal ones, wore blue facings and waistcoats. It had three brass buttons on each coat pocket and six on each cuff.

Régiment Languedoc was a relatively newer regiment, with blue facings and waistcoats. Three brass buttons were worn on each cuff.

Régiment Guyenne was raised in 1684. Facings and waistcoats were red, while three brass buttons were worn on each pocket and cuff.

Régiment Berry and Régiment Béarn were both also raised in 1684. Béarn had been formed from elements of the old Picardie Regiment. Both had red facings and waistcoats, the difference in the dress of the two being that Régiment Berry had five brass buttons on each cuff, while Béarn had only three. Both had three brass buttons on their pockets.

The arrangement of buttons on the coat, obviously, was quite important in telling the different regiments. All the buttons bore the regimental numbers, a feature first ordered about 1740.

*Note the hearts embroidered on the edges of the skirts, which hide the hooks and eyes used to pin the skirts out of the way when marching, on this officer's coat. Grenadier officers had grenades on theirs.*

*The French pakalem, or fatigue cap, was made from an old waistcoat, with binding, badge, and tassel made of white or yellow depending on the colour of the regimental buttons and hat lace.* (G. A. Embleton)

There were some further regimental dress distinctions for the grenadiers. Grenadiers were hand-picked from among the strongest and biggest men in each regiment and, at Ticonderoga, they were detached from their regiments and placed into a separate grenadier battalion. Grenadiers had earlier worn all-wool caps, not unlike bishops' mitres, with embroidered badges in front. Many regiments, however, began to use caps made of bearskin, which varied considerably in design from regiment to regiment. In 1763 bearskin caps were authorized for all the Army's grenadiers. Another dress distinction was at the point where the coat-tails were hooked together. Instead of the hearts used by fusiliers, cut from pieces of facing colour wool for enlisted men and embroidered for officers, grenadiers used flaming grenades.

Grenadiers were also encouraged to wear moustaches, while all the other men went clean-shaven. They carried broad-bladed, curved hangers, with red worsted sword-knots unique to grenadiers, instead of the other men's straight swords. The grenadier cartridge-box was also considerably larger than that of the other men.

In the old days, when grenadiers had actually thrown the iron balls filled with powder called grenades, these boxes carried their grenades. By this time, however, the boxes were fitted with wood blocks drilled out to hold cartridges. The grenadier's duty was about the same as the battalion man's, but he was still in an *élite* company.

It was a small Regular Army by European standards and one which suffered through being ignored by its government at home. The King's mistress made foreign policy, and her policy was to defeat Frederick of Prussia, and let the colonies do for themselves. What little in the way of supplies which were sent to the colonies fell into the hands of some of the greatest swindlers and thieves ever to hold important governmental offices.

The system was poor, many of the men at the top dishonest. But Montcalm was brave, intelligent, and resourceful, his men good and well-trained fighters. They held off defeat for a good number of years, more than any lesser army could have. They deserved better.

*The first of three ranks holds his musket in the position of 'Ready your arms', from which he can next aim and fire, or hold the weapon with bayonet out to defend himself.*

*In this position the firelock is ready, fully cocked, and the soldier can aim and fire.*

# 2

# The British Army 1753–1763

*General James Wolfe, as drawn around the battle of Quebec by an associate, wore a plain red frock-coat and carried a fusil for personal protection. The black armband is a sign of mourning for his recently dead father.* (Embleton/Osprey)

The British Army which would do battle for the American colonies was one which was recovering from an 'anti-army' attitude which had followed the great European wars of Marlborough. Its regiments, still bearing their colonels' names although numbers had been assigned to them in 1751, were stationed everywhere a British flag flew. Some were building roads in Scotland, some freezing in the wilds of North America, some living in tents in Gibraltar, still more sickening in the tropics.

This geographic spread led to quite a difference in dress, habits, and even drill between the regiments. James Wolfe, commanding the 20th Regiment of Foot, automatically expected to find differences between his and other regiments. In 1753 he inserted in orders, that:

'His royal highness the Duke when he reviewed the regiment at Reading was pleased to express his approbation of several parts of the discipline (i.e. drill) of it; such as the manner of carrying the arms, of levelling, of marching, and of wheeling, and in particular the silence and obedience that he observed, and ready compliance with orders, without the confusion sometimes perceived in the execution of things that seem new; but his Royal Highness thought that general Pultney's Regiment fired their platoons and subdivisions quicker than we did, wherefore lord Bury has commanded that we practise the same platoon exercise that they do; for to the difference between their platoon exercise and ours, his lordship ascribes their superiority in this point; and as his lordship is very desirous that no regiment should exceed his own in the performance of every part of their duty, and in matters of discipline, he desires we may begin to practise this platoon exercise as early as possible.'

Wolfe may have been the one who actually commanded the 20th in the field, but Lord Bury was its appointed colonel and it was his word which would decide what drill would be used. The appointed colonel rarely served with his regiment, being given the post largely as an honour for past services. He was also expected to profit from what money was left over after he met its annual expenses.

The regiment Lord Bury commanded, as with all British regiments, was made up of one grenadier and eight battalion companies. A typical regiment in America, the 15th Regiment of Foot, in 1760 had a lieutenant-colonel, a major, four captains, sixteen lieutenants, eight ensigns, a chaplain, an adjutant, a surgeon and his mate, a quartermaster, thirty-three sergeants, fourteen drummers, two fifers, and 455 rank and file, a total of 539 officers and men. It had left England with 858 officers and men. There were also six women per company, officially soldiers' wives, to do washing and mending.

According to the orderly book of the 44th Regiment of Foot, when in America in 1755: 'The Oldest Capts Company of each regt. is allways to Act as a Second Grendr: Compny And to be posted upon the left of the Battalion, leaving the same Intrival of

*This grenadier of the 15th Regiment of Foot wears his lapels buttoned half across for warmth, and his waistbelt over the coat. Because his regular cartridge-box carries so few cartridges, he has an extra one on a waistbelt. (Embleton/Osprey)*

*The faded pinkish-brown, heavy wool, foul-weather cloak worn by Wolfe. (National Army Museum)*

Lacing on the coats of grenadiers of the 43rd, 44th, and 45th Regiments would appear to have been designed largely on their colonels' whims, in this painting by David Morier. Gaiters were usually unbuttoned only a few buttons at top and bottom to slip on and off easily. (Reproduced by gracious permission of H.M. The Queen)

the Grends: upon the right. This Company to be Keept Complete of Officers & two of Them as well as of the other Grenr: Company are to be Posted in the Front & the other in the rear.'

As with the French, the grenadiers were the strongest, largest men in the regiment and their company was the *élite*. They, too, had thrown grenades in years past, but were now armed as and had the same combat duties as the battalion companies. When guards of honour were required, they were usually drawn from the grenadiers' ranks. When the whole regiment was drawn up, the grenadier company was usually posted on its right, in the post of honour. The major, mounted, led the grenadier company personally when on parade.

Although these arrangements were generally so, each regiment would set up its own formations. Wolfe told his regiment:

'The next time the regiment is under arms it is to be formed in the following order of battle by companies. Captain Beckwith's company upon the right of the battalion, with the colonel's company upon its left, makes up the right grand division under captain Beckwith's command; captain Wilkinson's company upon the left of the battalion, with the lieutenant-colonel's upon its right, makes the left

grand division of the regiment under captain Wilkinson's command; captain Maxwell's company upon the left of the colonel's, with the major's upon its left, makes the second grand division of the right wing of the battalion, under captain Maxwell's command; the duke of Richmond's company upon the right of the lieutenant-colonel's, with captain McDowall's upon its right, makes the second grand division of the left wing of the battalion under the duke of Richmond's command, or in his absence under captain McDowall's command – These eight companies are each to be told off into two platoons for the present; but they upon other occasions may only be considered as one platoon, if their numbers or other circumstances require it.

'The company of grenadiers is to be drawn up together upon the right of the battalion, and captain Grey's company as a piquet upon the left, each at a little distance from the battalion, and told off into two platoons.

'The officers are to be with their own companies: Where there are two captains in a grand division, one of them is to be in the rear, and one lieutenant is to be placed in the rear of each of the other grand divisions.

'One old soldier of each company (except the grenadiers) is to be chosen for the guard of the colours,

REGIMENT 46
REGIMENT 47
REGIMENT 48

*In 1751 a Swiss, David Morier, did a series of paintings for His Majesty of grenadiers of all the British regiments. Today, these are probably one of the best-known sources of period uniform information. This one shows grenadiers of the 46th, 47th, and 48th Regiments of Foot in full marching order. Note how high both the knapsack and haversack come under the men's arms.* (Reproduced by gracious permission of H.M. The Queen)

or a younger man of unexceptionable character for whose behaviour the captain will be answerable; these men are to be such as have never been punished for any crime, or even under sentence.

'This little platoon, with two sergeants, two corporals, supported by the hatchet-men (i.e. pioneers), are to guard and defend the colours, and a proper officer will be appointed to command them.'

Later Wolfe explained:

'Every grand division consisting of two companies, as they are now, is to be told off in three platoons, to be commanded by a captain, a lieutenant, and an ensign, with a sergeant to each; the rest of the officers and non-commissioned officers are to be distributed in the rear to compleat the files, to keep the men in their duty, and to supply the places of the sergeants that may be killed or dangerously wounded. The drummers are to stay with their respective companies to assist the wounded men.'

In action a regiment so drawn up would begin firing by platoons, either starting from the centre or from each flank. Each platoon would present (i.e. aim), fire, and immediately begin to reload. When halfway loaded, the next platoon would present, fire, and reload. In this way, each platoon would cover its neighbour, while the entire regiment belched forth a rolling and quite destructive fire.

A regiment need not fire this way only, however. At the Battle of Quebec, Wolfe had six regiments, each one standing three ranks deep. The French Army came at them on the double, stopping and firing a volley at some 130 yards, and then pressing on. When the French were only thirty paces away, Wolfe's troops, who had been standing motionless,

*This senior Royal Artillery officer, wears a uniform common to all ranks, but decorated with gold lace. Yellow lace on the other ranks' waistcoats was removed after 1758. While the officer wears the popular 'jockey' boots, other ranks wore black wool gaiters in the field and white ones on parade. Sergeants had two gold lace shoulder-knots; corporals, two worsted knots, and bombardiers, one.* (Embleton/Osprey)

*Line-regiment drummers wore facing colour coats, as this one of the 35th Regiment of Foot, with red facings. Guard and Royal Regiments wore the royal livery of red and blue. The coats in both cases were covered with regimental lace in any pattern the colonel chose.* (Embleton/Osprey)

silent, with shouldered arms, were suddenly ordered, as one entire unit, to poise, cock firelocks, present, give fire!

The entire line exploded in what was later called the most perfect volley ever fired. The French line disappeared, the French Army was destroyed in that single, smashing blow.

It was lucky for Wolfe that it was such a perfect volley. For had it been fired momentarily too soon or too late, or had the French a large enough force

26

with enough momentum, or had the volley been fired too high in the air or too low on the ground, nothing would have stopped the white-coated Regulars. The British would have had empty

Green jackets were used by men of Rogers' Rangers, along with grey coats. The blue Scottish bonnet was quite popular as many of the rangers came from the ranks of Scottish settlers. (Embleton/Osprey)

*A ranger of Goreham's company wears the uniform described by Captain John Knox of the 43rd Regiment of Foot in 1759. He also carries a quilled and tufted Indian pouch, along with an issue tin waterbottle and a tumpline, a type of Indian knapsack, with his kit inside. (Embleton/Osprey)*

weapons, with no time to load before the French would have closed to bayonet-fighting range.

Not that the British would have been frightened of crossing their iron triangular bayonets with those of the French. Wolfe told his regiment that on defence; 'They are to fix their bayonets and make a bloody resistance.' Night battles were fought more with bayonets than bullets, and all battles ended with a bayonet charge, one way or the other. The bayonet alone, however, was not sufficient to win wars. More

*A man of the 13th Regiment of Foot rams down his cartridge in this drawing by Lieutenant William Baillie, done in 1753. Note the hook and eye used to pull the coat-skirts together for ease of marching.* (Courtesy British Museum and Light Infantry Museum, Taunton)

important to the British troops was their firepower.

Firepower in the British infantry was provided by the Long Land Model Brown Bess Musket. It had a 0·75-calibre barrel, usually some forty-six inches long. Although there was a small rectangular stud on the muzzle, it was strictly a bayonet lug and not used as a sight. It was around the time of the Seven Years War that the steel ramrod was introduced into the British service. Dragoons used Short Land Model muskets, basically the same as the Long Land ones only with a forty-two-inch barrel. Long Land muskets given to the 42nd (Highland) Regiment of Foot were shortened to forty-two-inch barrels while in North America, too.

Wolfe pointed out that the officers should 'inform the soldiers of his platoon, before the action begins, where they are to direct their fire; and they are to take good aim to destroy their adversaries'. Furthermore, 'There is no necessity for firing very fast; a cool well leveled fire, with the pieces carefully loaded, is much more destructive and formidable than the quickest fire in confusion.'

As with the French muskets, there were some problems in handling the Long Land muskets.

'There are some particulars in relation to fire-arms that the soldiers should know,' [advised Wolfe].

'One is, the quantity of powder that throws a ball out of a musket in the truest direction to the mark, and to the greatest distance; a matter that experience and practice will best discover; soldiers are apt to imagine that a great quantity of powder has the best effect, which is a capital error. The size of the cartridge with ball is another material consideration, because when the musket grows foul with repeated firing, a ball too near the calibre of the musket will not go down without great force, and the danger of firing the piece when the ball is not rammed well home is well known (i.e. the musket will blow up): the soldiers should be informed that no other force in ramming down a charge is necessary than to collect the powder and place the ball close upon it. If the ball is rammed too hard upon the powder, a great part of it will not take fire, and consequently the shot will be of so much the less force.'

Besides muskets, cannon added to the British Army's firepower. North America, being mostly a wilderness, however, artillery's use in the war was limited. In 1758 an artillery train under Colonel Williamson was part of the force Wolfe used to capture Louisbourg, and brought down some of the fort's walls. At the battle of Quebec some fifty artillerymen and two guns of Captain Macleod's company were present, and Captain-Lieutenant Yorke received commendation for his use of the light artillery there.

The Royal Artillerymen themselves wore their traditional dress of blue coats with red lapels, collars, and cuffs. Their coats were trimmed with yellow lace, as were their waistcoats. Waistcoats and breeches were red wool, about the same weight as the wool of their coats. Their tricorne hats were bound up with yellow wool worsted tape, or lace. They carried Brown Besses for personal defence, their cartridges being carried in small black cartridge-boxes worn on their waistbelts over their stomachs.

Officers wore similar uniforms with gold lace and gilt buttons. Often they wore boots. As with all British officers, a crimson silk net sash was worn over the right shoulder, knotted on the left hip. Their gorgets were gilt.

Cannon used in the war were pretty small, and the war in America must be considered basically an infantryman's war.

The wilderness, and the way Indians chose to

fight, led to the creation of a new type of infantry, the light infantry. Probably the first especially designated light infantrymen in the British service were those answering an advertisement in the *Boston Weekly News Letter* of 4 October 1750.

'All Gentlemen Volunteers and Others That have a mind to serve his Majesty King GEORGE the Second, for a limited Time in the Independent Companies of Rangers now in *Nova-Scotia*, may apply to Lieutenant *Alexander Collender*, at Mr. *Jonas Leonard's*, at the Sign of the *Lamb* at the South End of *Boston*, where they shall be kindly entertained, enter into present Pay, and have good quarters, and when they join their respective Companies in *Hallifax*, shall be completely cloathed in blue Broad-Cloth, receive Arms, Accoutrements, Provisions,

*Major Robert Rogers wears the uniform of his battalion of rangers in this contemporary mezzotint. He carries a fusil and wears a cap probably cut down from an issue tricorne.*
(John Ross Robertson Collection, Metropolitan Toronto Central Library)

and all other things necessary for a Gentleman Ranger. . . .'

The rangers fought a constant guerrilla war during the years between the Treaty of Aix-la-Chapelle and the beginning of the Seven Years War along the Canadian frontier. Fighting without benefit of drums, colours, or glorious speeches, they had built up quite a record by the war's formal beginning.

The 'old company', the first company organized, was led by John Goreham. It was recruited from among qualified woodsmen taken from the New Englanders sent by Governor Shirley to Annapolis Royal in 1743. They considered themselves not provincials but regulars, serving directly under the King. Goreham's younger brother, Joseph, succeeded command of the company by 1758, and performed well at Louisbourg. Wolfe took six ranger companies with him to Quebec. Goreham is said to have commanded 'The Corps of Rangers', carried in the period *Army Lists* as the 'North American Rangers'.

The rangers may have considered themselves and been listed as regulars, but any fussy fops at St James would have been hard put to so recognize them. Captain Knox wrote that they wore regular issue uniforms, 'cut short'. In Loudoun's papers in 1757 an entry states that: 'The Irregulars in Nova Scotia are Payed on the Regular Troops are cloathed by the Board of Trade and have Leather Caps. They have powderhorns in place of Cartridge Boxes.'

In May, 1759, however, Knox noted that:

'The rangers have got a new uniform clothing; the ground is of black ratteen or frize, lapelled and cuffed with blue; here follows a description of their dress; a waistcoat with sleeves; a short jacket without sleeves; only armholes and wings to the shoulders (in like manner as the Grenadiers and Drummers of the army) white metal buttons, linen or canvas drawers, with a blue skirt or petticoat of stuff, made with a waistband and one button; this is open before and does not quite extend to the knees; a pair of leggins of the same colour with their coat, which reach up to the middle of the thighs (without flaps) and from the calf of the leg downwards they button like spatter-dashes; and this active dress they wear blue bonnets, and, I think, in great measure like our Highlanders.'

Each regiment had its own light infantry company. Coats were made without sleeves, but with wings which covered the waistcoat sleeves and made them look like coat sleeves. Two special leather pockets were sewn on coats to carry extra flints and balls. The caps had black wool flaps, which could be hooked shut around the chin for warmth, or hooked out of the way on top of the cap. (Embleton/Osprey)

The dark brown coats of the 80th Regiment of Light Armed Foot, as worn by this private, were probably the regiment's first issue. The unit appears to have received a variety of dress, probably according to what was available at the time. (Embleton/Osprey)

*Even dress of battalion men was affected by frontier warfare.*
*This private of the 55th Regiment of Foot in 1758 wears the*
*modifications of his uniform ordered by its colonel, Lord Howe.*
(Embleton/Osprey)

*The ensign of the 44th Regiment of Foot, wearing the dress*
*uniform of that regiment, holds its Regimental Colour, a*
*six-foot-square silk banner of facing colour. The King's*
*Colour was the other flag used by a regiment, and that was the*
*Union flag, with a wreath of thistles and roses and a regimental*
*number in the centre.* (Embleton/Osprey)

Back of Captain Plumbe's uniform, showing its gold lace and copper-gilt buttons. Gaiters are of white linen, with a linen tape running under the shoe and twenty-nine horn buttons up each leg.

The full uniform of Captain Thomas Plumbe, Royal Lancashire Militia, c. 1760. The uniform is red, the coat and waistcoat being lined, the latter only partially, in blue; and blue velvet was used to line the collar.

Given the active campaigning of the rangers, any dress would be quick to wear out. In 1761 Goreham wrote Jeffery Amherst that many of his officers were unfit for duty because of their hard service and wounds. In that same year five men of his own company deserted, possibly because of the hard campaigning, in dress quite different than that Captain Knox described. Said an advertisement in the *Boston News Letter*, describing the deserters: 'The above Persons were clothed in the Uniform of the Company, viz, Coats red turn'd up with brown, with brown Capes and brown Insides, which may be worn either Side out; Waistcoats of the brown Colour; Linnen Draws; leather Jockey-Caps, with Oak-Leaf or Branch painted on the left Side. . . .'

More famous than Goreham's Rangers were those of Robert Rogers. This company was neither regular nor provincial, although Rogers tried to get it placed on the regular establishment. It was paid directly by the King, and listed as: 'His Majesty's Independent Companies of American Rangers.' Rogers had five companies, each consisting of a captain, two lieutenants, one ensign, four sergeants, and a hundred privates. An Indian company was also raised for his command, as one of the companies.

The Indians wore their own dress, while the men were merely to have good, warm clothing as uniform as possible in each company. Rogers tried also to get the government to supply them with uniforms, but his pleas fell on deaf ears. Two of the companies, therefore, wore grey duffle coats and greatcoats, while the other two wore green jackets or hunting-shirts.

The hunting-shirt was a unique American invention. It was basically the same as the farmer's frock of Europe, made either to pull over or open all the way, of linen. Usually, several linen capes were a part of the shirt, and they could be pulled over the head to protect against bad weather. As a decoration, most men fringed their hunting-shirts, usually around the edges and with several bands of fringing around the arms. Plain buckskin hunting-shirts were also worn.

Like all rangers, Rogers' men were rather individualists. They could not be as easily disciplined as regulars, and therefore, Rogers' regimental orders, issued in 1759, were simple and to the point:

'Don't forget nothing. Have your musket clean as a whistle, tomahawk scoured, sixty rounds powder and ball, and be ready to march at a moment's notice. When you're on the march, act the way you would if you were sneaking up on a deer, see the enemy first.

'Tell the truth about what you see and what you do. There is an army depending on us for correct information. You can lie all you please when you tell other folks about the Rangers, but don't lie to a Ranger or officer.

'Don't never take a chance you don't have to. When we're on the march we march single file far enough apart so one shot can't go through two men. If we strike swamps, or soft ground, we spread out abreast, so it's hard to track us. When we march, we keep moving till dark, so as to give the enemy the least possible chance at us.

'When we camp, half the party stays awake, while the other half sleeps. If we take prisoners we keep 'em separate 'till we have time to examine them so they can't cook up a story between them.

'Don't ever march home the same way. Take a different route so you won't be ambushed. Each party has to keep a scout 20 yards head, 20 yards on each flank and 20 yards in the rear so the main body can't be wiped out. Every night you'll be told where to meet if surrounded by a superior force. Don't sit down to eat without posting sentries. Don't sleep beyond dawn, dawn's when the French and Indians attack. Don't cross a river by a regular ford. If somebody's trailing you make a circle, come back on your own tracks, and ambush the folks that's aimin' to ambush you.

'Don't stand up when the enemy's aiming at you; kneel down, lie down, or hide behind a tree. Let the enemy come till he's almost close enough to touch, then let him have it and jump up and finish him up with your tomahawk.'

Certainly this sort of informality would not satisfy the requirements of a major war, and the Captain-General of the Army, the Duke of Cumberland, wrote that 'till *Regular* Officers with men that they can trust, learn to beat the woods, & act as *Irregulars*, you will never gain any certain Intelligence of the Enemy'. That note, followed quickly by a sloppy, undisciplined scouting party of rangers in November 1757 and a small mutiny of other Rangers, caused John Campbell, Earl of Loudoun, the new Massachusetts governor, to be interested in training regular troops to serve as rangers.

When, therefore, Lieutenant-Colonel Thomas Gage, of the 44th Regiment of Foot, and fresh from Braddock's disaster, suggested to Loudoun that he could raise and clothe at his own expense, a regiment of 500 regular rangers, the suggestion was eagerly accepted. Recruiters were sent as far south as Virginia and by the summer of 1758 his regiment, the 80th Regiment of Light-Armed Foot, was ready for service.

Men were easily recruited from among competent woodsmen interested in fighting, but not in the regular regimental discipline. Getting good officers was another matter. Few good officers wanted to transfer to a regiment which would obviously be stood down on the war's end, naturally preferring to get into the oldest regiments they could. Moreover, the type of duty rangers had to perform was so different, so much more exacting in many ways than that of other regiments, that many officers simply weren't up to it.

*A typical battalion private wears his hat at such a jaunty angle to prevent it from being knocked off by his musket during drill.* (Courtesy British Museum and Light Infantry Museum, Taunton)

None the less, the regiment had twenty-one officers and 454 other ranks present by 1760. It saw much good service, fighting in the Ticonderoga area.

Since the regiment's duties involved stalking about in dense woods, red coats such as worn by other regiments, were fairly unreasonable. Instead, the regiment wore brown coats initially, with the facings changed from year to year, depending on

*Braddock's men rapidly converted their uniforms to meet American necessities, as this private of the 48th has already done. His small clothes are linen, his gaiters brown canvas, and his sword has been left in stores. His cartridge-box has had its straps removed and resewn as a waistbelt box. (Embleton/Osprey)*

supply. In the official Lace Book of November 1758 the regiment is described as wearing 'Dark Brown Short Coats; Linings dark brown; no lace; Buttons . . . Black'. In a list of British regiments published in New York in 1761, the regimental uniform was, 'Light Brown Jacketts, faced White, flat Yellow Buttons'.

At any rate, the brown coat was worn by both men and officers. In 1760 an officer of the Highland Regiment of Foot, Captain Allen Campbell, mentioned that his nephew, who had transferred to the 80th, '. . . was under a necessity of Buying new Regimentals, as these Differ in Colours from the rest of the Army, being Brown'.

Along with the brown coats, the men received, according to a December 1757 clothing estimate, waistcoats, breeches, leggings, hatchets with handles, knives with sheaths, shoes, stockings, flannel shirts, shot-bags, horns, and 'Capps'. Originally they carried Long Land Model Brown Besses, but in May 1759 they were 'to receive this Day a Compleat Sett of Carbines without Bayonets for that Regt. being 520 . . .'. The new carbines were to have barrels 'made blue or brown, to take off the glittering'.

Perhaps all these innovations at once were too much for conservative military minds. Men of the 80th began to receive red coats, instead of brown, as early as 1760. That year the annual *Army List* gives the 80th red coats faced 'orange-brown', the facings changing next year to 'plum-colour', or yellow, and back to orange-brown by 1763. An original painting of an officer of the 80th shows golden-coloured facings.

In 1763, at the war's end, the 80th was stood down. But its teachings were to be far-reaching on the British Army.

Regiments began forming light infantry companies themselves. The 1st Battalion the Royal Scots Regiment of Foot even had a light company when stationed in Ireland in 1763, although this company like those of all the other regiments, was stood down that year. The colonel commanding the King's Own Regiment of Foot, in Guadeloupe, had the best marksmen of his regiment formed into a special light company, and this company, along with the other light companies, was formed into a separate light battalion.

Not only were regiments adapting to woodland warfare by forming light companies, but by chang-

*A knot of white tape on this man's right shoulder shows that he is a corporal in the 45th Regiment of Foot. In all other respects, he wears the typical basic battalion man's uniform. (Embleton/Osprey)*

ing their own battalion tactics and dress. Stories of British troops refusing to face the new realities of war in America, of stiff, red-coated lines of regulars firing wasted volleys after elusive Indians are just that – stories.

A young girl who had seen the 55th Regiment of regulars firing wasted volleys after elusive Indians wrote that

'they were . . . considered as an example to the whole [British] American Army . . . [the unit's colonel] forbade all displays of gold and scarlet . . . and set the example by wearing himself an ammunition [private man's] coat . . . one of the surplus soldier's coats cut short . . . he ordered the muskets to be shortened . . . the barrels of their guns were all blackened . . . he set the example of wearing leggins . . . Lord Howe's [hair] was fine and very abundant; he, however, cropped it, and ordered everyone else to do the same.'

A surgeon, writing home, agreed with this description

'The Art of War is much changed and improved here. I suppose by the end of the summer it will have undergone a total Revolution. We are now literally an army of round Heads. Our hair is about an inch long; the Flaps of our Hats, which are wore slouched, about two inches and a half broad. Our Coats are docked rather shorter than the Highlanders. . . . The Highlanders have put on Breeches and Lord How's Filabegs. Some from an affection to their Gorgets still wear them. Swords and Sashes are degraded and many have taken up the Hatchet and wear Tomahawks.'

The move to comfort was well received by officers and men. An officer wrote home: 'You would laugh to see the droll figure we all cut. Regulars and provincials are ordered to cut off the brims of their hats. The regulars as well as the provincials have left off their proper regimentals, that is, they have cut their coats so as to scarcely reach their waist. You would not distinguish us from common plough men.'

The men who arrived at first in America would hardly have been mistaken for common ploughmen. They were men of the 44th, Halkett's, Regiment of Foot and the 48th, Dunbar's, Regiment of Foot. Both regiments had been present, and fled from, the

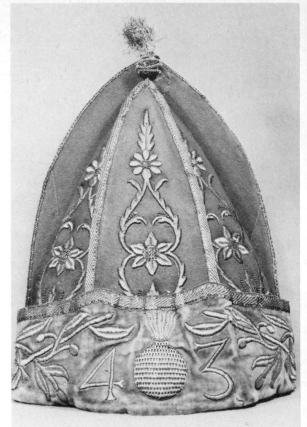

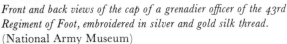

*Front and back views of the cap of a grenadier officer of the 43rd Regiment of Foot, embroidered in silver and gold silk thread.* (National Army Museum)

field at Prestonpans during the 1745 rebellion, so neither could have been considered the best the country had to offer.

'Best' regiments or not, their appearance should have been enough to strike fear into the most brave of Indians, courage into the most scared of colonials. The men wore brick-red wool coats, with yellow cuffs, lapels, and linings for the 44th, buff for the 48th. The coats were made without collars, and liberal portions of worsted wool lace with different-coloured designs for the different regiments, were sewn around buttonholes, lapels, pockets, and cuffs. Waistcoats were also laced.

Shirts were white linen for dress and blue or black and white check for fatigue. Long white linen stocks were tightly pulled around their necks. Waistcoats and breeches were of the same heavy, hot red wool

as were their coats. Royal regiments had blue wool breeches and waistcoats. Long white linen gaiters, closed with dozens of small buttons, were pulled over black leather shoes, fastened with brass buckles, and cloth stockings. Gaiters were quite tight, but still had to be held up with black leather garter-belts buckled at the back.

Battalion men wore large black felt tricornes, pointed equally at all three sides, and bound up with white wool worsted tape. Grenadiers, on the other hand, wore caps, like French grenadiers. These were made of wool, about a foot tall. Some regiments were allowed special regimental designs on their caps, according to traditions. Most, however, used caps with a facing colour wool front, edged in white tape. A royal cipher, GR, was embroidered in white worsted, on top of which was a crown, done in

*Front and back views of the cap of a grenadier private of the 49th Regiment of Foot, bound in white tape. This cap is less embroidered than that of the officer.* (National Army Museum)

correct colours. Leaves were embroidered in white worsted on each side of the cipher. Below all this display was a small false front of red wool, edged in white with the motto *Nec Asper Terrent* (Hardships do not frighten them) and a white running horse.

The headband was also in facing colour wool, with a 'bag' of red wool forming the cap's insides. A white flaming grenade was embroidered on the back centre of the headband, and a regimental number appeared on each side of that. A tassel of facing colour and white worsted on top finished off the whole thing.

In a light-coloured regiment, such as the 48th with buff facings, the embroidery on the caps was green.

All the men carried large cartridge-boxes, made more like a pouch than a box, with a wood block

inside bored out to hold twenty-four cartridges. It was suspended by a wide buff leather belt, with two brass buckles near the box and one in the centre of the chest. A pick and brush was hung from the flap below the front buckle. The pick was used to clear the musket's touch-hole, while the brush cleaned out its pan.

Grenadiers wore a pierced brass tube, closed with a wooden end, on their cartridge-box slings. These held matches, which had been used to light grenades. Although grenades were no longer in use, the match-cases were retained as symbols of the men's status.

The bayonet was suspended on a buff waistbelt, slightly narrower than the cartridge-box sling, with two frogs. The second frog held the bayonet, and the first held the soldier's hanger. These were usually plain, brass-hilted swords, although a wide variety

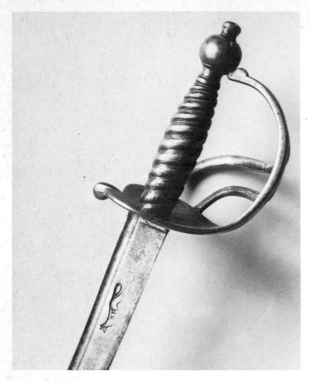

*This brass-hilted 1751-pattern hanger is marked by the running wolf and SH of its British maker.* (G. A. Embleton)

of hanger styles is known. They had plain, dull blades usually between twenty-four and thirty inches long.

Water was carried in a tin waterbottle, hung on a plain rope. Each man was to carry some six days' rations in a haversack of grey or natural-coloured canvas, hanging on the right side on top of the cartridge-box. In action, it was pushed behind the box.

His spare clothing was carried in a cowhide, furry knapsack, hung with the waterbottle on his left side.

The cartridge-box, pushed so far back on his hip, was not very easy to get to, and it became the practice, just before action, for each man to reach into the box of the man on his left, pull out a couple of rounds, and give them to him. These rounds would then be tucked into his breeches' waistband, easy to get to quickly.

This entire load was anything but well designed for the type of fighting His Majesty's men would have to do in America. Lieutenant Alexander Baillie, 1st Battalion, 60th Regiment of Foot, figured out its weight and reported it to his colonel in August, 1762.

'Return of the Weight of the Cloathing, Arms, Accoutrements, Ammunition, Provision, Necessary's &Ca. of a Grenadier, upon a March.

|  | Weight lbs. | Qrs. |
|---|---|---|
| 'A Regimental Coat with Hooks, Eyes, &ca. | 5. | 2. |
| Waistcoat | 2. | 1. |
| Pair of Breeches | 1. | 2. |
| Hat with cockade, Button, Loop, & Hair String | 1. | — |
| A shirt with Sleeve Buttons | 1. | — |
| A Stock with a Buckle |  |  |
| A Pair Knee Buckles | — | 3. |
| A Pair Stockings & Garters |  |  |
| A Pair Shoes with Buckles | 1. | 2. |
| A Regimental Firelock, with a Sling & Buckle Hammer Cap & Stopper | 11. | 1. |
| A Waist Belt with a Buckle | — | 2. |
| A Hanger, Sword Knot, and Scabbord | 2. | 3. |
| A Bayonet and Scabbord | 2. | 1. |
| A Tomahawk, and Cover | 1. | 3. |
| A Cartridge Pouch with Belt, Buckles, & Match Case | 3. | — |
| Containing 24 Cartridges | 2. | 1 |
| Brush, Wire, Worm, and Turnkey Oyl Bottle & Rag | — | 1. |
| 2 Flints, & a Steel |  |  |
| A Knapsa(ck) with Strap, & Buckles | 1. | 2. |
| Containing 2 Shirts |  |  |
| 2 Stocks | 2. | 3. |
| 2 Pair Stockings |  |  |
| A Pair Summer Breeches | 1. | 1. |
| A Pair Shoes | 1. | 1. |
| A Clothes Brush, pair Shoe Brushes and a Black Ball | 1. | — |
| A Pair Leggins & Garters |  |  |
| A Hankerchief | 1. | 1. |
| 2 Combs, a Knife & Spoon | — | 2. |
| A Haversack, with a Strap | — | 3. |
| Containing Six Days Provisions | 10. | 1. |
| A Blanket with Strap & Harters | 3. | 2. |
| A Canteen with a String & Stopper, full of water | 3. | 1. |
| (GROSS WEIGHT) | 63. | 3.' |

This was obviously too much for the poor soldier to bear; that fact was immediately evident. On 19 April 1755 General Braddock wrote of his men that he had '. . . lighten'd them as much as possible, and have left in store their Swords and the greatest part of their heavy Accoutrements.'

As in the French Army, swords were certainly the first thing to go, and in 1759 an order came out of headquarters in America ordering the 'sergeants to carry firelocks, instead of halberds, with cartouche box and bayonet instead of sword, the soldiers no swords nor sword belt, if they can take their bayonet securely without them; . . . the Grenadiers to take their swords into the field . . . the Royal Highland Regiment and the 77th Highlanders are excepted in the order of no swords. The C.O. of each of those regiments may do as he thinks best.'

British halberds were made with a spear-point and axe combination head, and, as the sergeants turned them in, many officers exchanged their spontoons for muskets. Officers, besides, were 'to do all Dutys in boots And never any plain Hatts and Gloves Allways'. Washington, serving with the Army, wrote home: 'As wearing boots is quite the mode and mine in a declining state, I must beg you to procure me a pair that is good and neat.'

Both weapons and uniforms were turned in to cut down on the weight. In the 44th Regiment of Foot, it was ordered that 'the Officers Are to see their men Comply with the Orders of the 8th of April (Viz) to leave their Shoulder Bellts & Wast Bellts And Hangers behind And only are to take with Them to the field one spair Shirt one spair pair of stockins one spair pair of socs And one pair of Brown Gaiters.'

Besides weight, the heat of wool uniforms in America was a problem. The men were issued light-weight oznaburg, a type of duck linen, breeches and waistcoats. They were also given thin leather pads, called bladders, to put in between

*This private of the 42nd (Highland) Regiment of Foot in 1758 wears his regiment's full dress. In the field, linen breeches and gaiters were often worn on fatigue duties. (Embleton/Osprey)*

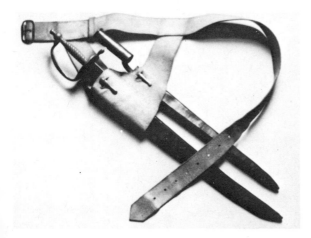

*Reconstruction from an original of a whitened buff leather waistbelt, fifty-two inches long, holding a 1742 pattern hanger and Brown Bess bayonet. (Author's collection)*

their hats' linen linings and black felt crowns to protect them from the sun.

Another change from wars in Europe was the observation that the rifle was an excellent weapon to have when fighting Indians in the woods, where accuracy was more important than speed of loading. Some twelve rifles, with bullet-moulds, were issued to the 44th and 48th, while in 1758, '10 Rifled Barrelled Guns were delivered out to each regiment to be put into the hands of their best Marksmen. . . .' Exactly what sort of rifles these were is a matter open to debate. They may have been German Jäger rifles, short-barrelled, heavy weapons, firing a large, almost musket-sized ball. These would have had to have been sent from England. Although an accurate weapon, they were at some disadvantage to the weapon developed by German gunsmiths on the frontiers of Pennsylvania.

It may be that this latter gun, locally procured, is what the troops received. These were long, slender and graceful weapons, firing quite small balls. The reason for the small ball was so that the pioneer, far away from supplies, could carry much more ammunition with him than he could, were the balls large and heavy.

Both rifles were pin-fastened, the Pennsylvania ones being made with iron as well as brass furniture. As they were apt to be the most valuable thing the pioneer owned, they were often beautifully decorated.

Rifles were not the only different weapons in the Army. Scottish Highlanders were uniquely armed. Highlanders, considered by many English to be as savage as the American Indians, had been recently formed into British fighting units. The first of these was the 42nd, the Highland Regiment. It had been sent to America in 1756 and two years later had been so destroyed in an almost superhuman attempt to take Fort Ticonderoga, losing 314 officers and men dead, 333 more wounded, that His Majesty granted it the designation of the Royal Highland Regiment.

The 42nd was followed by two newly raised regiments, Montgomery's Highlanders, the 77th Regiment, which arrived in 1758, and Fraser's Highlanders, the 78th Regiment. Fraser's was officially raised as the 2nd Highland Regiment of Foot.

A fully armed Highlander was almost as well armed as a modern battleship. Besides his shortened Brown Bess, he carried a long, basket-hilted broadsword suspended on a wide black belt worn from his right shoulder to his left hip. From the same shoulder a small belt carried a metal-stocked pistol, either of brass or iron. Many men and probably all officers and sergeants carried dirks, although the bayonet was considered sufficient for most fights. The broadsword, however, was carried by all ranks and, indeed, was often preferred in combat to the musket and bayonet.

The bayonet was suspended from the waistbelt, along with a small cartridge-box, usually plain but sometimes painted with the Royal Crown and the letters, GR.

The uniform, too, was a variation from the English one. Grenadiers wore bearskin caps, with red and white front plates bearing the Royal Cypher. Battalion men wore low blue bonnets, with red bands and a piece of bearskin on the left side.

Waistcoats, which were worn by themselves in the American hot weather, were red wool, trimmed with regimental lace. Coats were also red, made without lapels, cut quite short, with yellow collar and cuffs for the 42nd. The 77th wore green facings, the 78th white. When the 42nd was made a Royal regiment, the men were not altogether happy about changing their yellow for blue facings, red and yellow being the ancient colours of Scotland. Indeed, so far from supplies, it is most likely that, for quite some time after they were to change into blue facings, they simply wore blue armbands or similar marks to indicate their being Royal.

The men originally wore the great belted plaid, a giant piece of material put on by lying flat on the ground and rolling oneself up in it. Gradually this had given way to the *feilidh beag*, the little kilt, which was a kilt simply buckled shut. A separate piece of material, the fly plaid, was worn around the waist and buttoned on the left shoulder, serving as the cloak in cool weather.

All Highland regiments used the government sett tartan, the modern Black Watch tartan, which had been taken from a Campbell tartan for use by the 42nd from its first days. One contemporary illustration of a grenadier in 1758 shows him with a thin red stripe overlaid on his plaid, and this has led to great debates. It has been suggested that this was a special plaid just for the grenadier company. An early historian of the 42nd suggested it was used on the *feilidh beag* to differentiate that from the great belted plaid. Probably the most likely suggestion offered is that the man was simply stood down from a previously raised regiment, Loudoun's Highlanders, and wore his old kilt.

Like the rest of the Army, Highlanders made uniform changes for the American service. Canvas breeches and blue leggings were often worn instead of kilts for boat duty and field work. Officers, in fact, generally wore linen breeches, and removed most of their lace from coats and waistcoats.

The Highlanders were not the only recently raised organizations sent to America. With a war being fought in two theatres, units were badly needed and in 1760 some lieutenants were encouraged to submit letters of proposal to raise companies 'for rank'. Each would become the company captain, who could appoint lieutenants from officers then on active service and ensigns from among their civilian friends. The new captains would continue to be listed on their regimental rosters while recruiting, as on leave, but they would not receive their new commissions until the companies were completed and mustered. By this method, never tried before, some sixty-two independent companies were raised by November 1760.

Since these companies were not to be put into regular regiments, a standard dress of coats of 'Scarlet, lined with Scarlet, with white buttons, & without lace', was ordered.

The companies were divided into divisions of six companies each, the senior captain acting as divisional commander. The first two divisions were sent to America in late 1760, landing in New York, and were later sent to South Carolina.

The idea of independent companies may have been a good one for raising troops quickly, but they turned out not to be a very useful combat-size unit, and in 1761 they were all placed into new regiments numbered 95 to 120. The two divisions in America were designated the 95th Regiment of Foot, and their plain red coats were changed to ones 'to be faced with a light Grey and laced with a mix'd Lace of white and Green . . . to be Lapell'd as by his Majesty's Regulation'. Serving in the hot south, the troops were allowed to have linen coat-linings, breeches, and stockings instead of wool.

Grey, although a handsome facing colour, was certainly an unusual one. In 1761 a list of troops serving in America indicated that the 1st Regiment had blue facings, as did the 42nd, 60th (Royal American), and 94th (Royal Welsh Volunteers). Buff facings were worn by the 22nd, 27th (Inniskillings), 40th, and 48th. Yellow, a popular facing colour, was worn by the 15th, 28th, 44th, and 46th. The 17th, 43rd, 47th, and 78th Regiments wore white facings. The 35th Regiment wore orange, a difficult colour to dye then. Green facings were worn by the 45th, 55th, and 77th Regiments. The 58th wore black facings.

Not that each regiment was identical in everything but facings. The 94th, for example, wore a white strap on each shoulder. The 60th had no lace on their coats or waistcoats at all.

'Popinger green' is the facing colour worn by the three independent South Carolina Companies which had been formed before the war from the disbanded Oglethorpe's Regiment of Foot. Men of these companies were with Washington at Fort

*Among other interesting details on the coat of the Highland Regiment's grenadier, is that the collar is sewn to the coat below the strip of lace around the neck. The controversial red stripe on the kilt also appears in this painting. (Reproduced by gracious permission of H.M. The Queen)*

Necessity, and later with Braddock. Thereafter, they were transferred to the 50th Regiment, while the officers returned to South Carolina to recruit. By 1757 the three companies were back to normal strength. One of the companies surrendered at Fort Loudoun in 1760.

Nor were these companies the only ones recruited in South Carolina. In 1757 the colonial legislature authorized raising the South Carolina Provincial Regiment, to consist of seven companies, each with 100 privates. The regiment never exceeded 500 men, however, and in 1759 it was officially made a three-company regiment.

Perhaps as a mark to show that these were provincials, not British regulars, they did not wear red coats. Instead, each man was issued with a blue wool coat, with buff cuffs and linings, buff wool waistcoats, and blue wool breeches. Each man also had a white laced tricorne, white thread stockings, a pair of shoes, a musket, bayonet, belt, and cartridge-box.

The other colonies, richer, larger and certainly closer to the seat of the war than South Carolina, would have to raise regiments, too, even if their pennypinching legislatures didn't like it. Regulars certainly could not be everywhere, and slowly each colony raised provincial units to defend themselves.

Massachusetts militiamen received blue coats faced red, and red or blue wool breeches, as well as 'a soldier's hat'. The Massachusetts Regiment was also about 500 strong, divided into companies of fifty.

New Jersey's regiment was also in blue faced red, giving them the nickname of the 'Jersey Blues'. The Act which authorized this 1,000-strong regiment, passed in 1755, stated that 'the said company will purchase or procure for each Volunteer the following clothing or other articles to be delivered unto them respectively at the time of muster or embarkation, to wit, a blue coat after the Highland manner, lappelled and cuffed with red, one pair ticken breeches, one pair of blue ditto of the same cloth as the coat, one check shirt, one white ditto, 2 pairs of yarn stockings, 2 pairs of shoes, one hat to each man bound with yellow bindings, one blanket, one knapsack, one hatchet, one canteen, one kettle to five men, a pair of white spatterdashes, and also one hundred grenadier caps for 100 of said soldiers, 200 felling axes for the whole regiment.' The

regiment, after gaining a reputation for its good discipline and behaviour at such battles as Oswego and Ticonderoga, was demobilized in 1763.

The same year the Jersey Blues were created, the New York legislature raised a regiment of eight companies of 100 men each to build forts around Crown Point. They offered: 'To each able bodied and effective man who shall voluntarily inlist himself, a good blanket, together with a good lappelled

*This private of one of the South Carolina independent companies has buttoned his coat across his chest, with just a bit of the green facings showing. His coat is lined in linen instead of wool, because of that colony's hot weather. (Embleton/Osprey)*

The 'Jersey Blues', of which this man is a member, were probably the best-known of the provincial regiments raised. His uniform colours are the same as those of his colonel, Philip Schuyler, painted in his full regimental uniform, but his coat has been cut short, after the Highland manner, as ordered. He is regarding a slightly fringed smock, which is buttoned at the cuff, unlike the hunting-shirt, and lacks the capes of the typical hunting-shirt. (Embleton/Osprey)

up with middle drab cloth, buckskin breeches and waistcoat, dark worsted stockings, new shoes and an old hat'.

The colour of drab is, again, a debatable subject. Definitions given of it around the time, however, simply state that it is a type of heavy, woollen cloth, and fail to mention any actual colour. Probably, therefore, the coat was a natural, tannish colour, undyed, as was often the case in cheaply made coats of the period.

coat, a felt hat, one shirt, two pr oznaburg trousers, one pair of shoes, one pair of stockings.' The early New York troops, however, were mostly encouraged to show up in civilian clothes and not expect uniforms. In a description of a deserter of 1757, however, a uniform is mentioned, 'a New York regimented coat which is dark drab, the sleeves turned

Connecticut supplied three regiments, mostly dressed in similar styles. This officer is closely copied from a painting of Colonel Nathan Whiting, 2nd Connecticut, who commanded one of the colony's battalions at Ticonderoga in 1758. (Embleton/Osprey)

*Edward Penny, in 1765, painted this version of the death of General Wolfe from an eyewitness account. In the distance the British have advanced and are firing, the first rank kneeling. Uniforms appear quite accurately done.* (Courtesy the Ashmolean Museum, Oxford)

Pennsylvania was very slow in raising troops, because its subjects were mostly Quakers or Germans of various pacifist religious sects. Nonetheless, in November 1755, militia companies were authorized. The following year two battalions of the Pennsylvania Regiment were raised. The first was made up of the companies west of the Susquehanna River, which runs north and south through the state some 100 miles west of Philadelphia. The second, of those east of the river. A third battalion was then raised to build and garrison Fort Augusta.

Later these designations were changed to the 1st (Augusta) Regiment and the 2nd (Pennsylvania) Regiment. In 1758 twenty-three new companies were raised, and sixteen of them put into a new third battalion of the Pennsylvania Regiment.

In 1757 the men, who had been wearing their own clothes, were ordered into green coats, red waistcoats, and buckskin breeches. One man, objecting to this, wrote: 'Must the men buy green Cloathing? I fear this will hurt us much. I think linnen Stockings, red below the Knee, Petticoat Trousers, reaching to the thick of the Leg, made of Strong Linnen, and a Sailor's Frock made of the same, would be best. Young men that have Cloathing (especially Dutch) will not like to lay out their Money for more.'

This logical suggestion seems to have been ignored, and a typical deserter description of a man of the 1st Battalion in 1759 has the men in

44

'their regimental coats, green cloth faced with red, red waistcoats and buckskin breeches'. The companies raised for the 2nd battalion mostly wore 'short green coats, lapell'd with the same'. It would appear likely that the 1st Battalion had red facings, the 2nd green. At any rate, by 1759–61 the green coats were exchanged for blue, probably with blue facings.

Each battalion of the Pennsylvania Regiment had one company turned into a light horse troop in 1759. They received cavalry accoutrements and weapons, but at least one regular officer didn't think much of them. 'The sabres, or rather hangers, which were given to the light cavalry are a joke. It is their principal weapon and they could not kill a chicken with this tiny knife.'

Other equipment supplied by the colony was equally bad. Muskets were rusty, their stocks often cracked and repaired with string. Recruits, therefore, were encouraged to bring their own weapons, and many brought Pennsylvania rifles.

It was the troops of one colony – Virginia – which had started the war which were now causing the other colonies to raise regiments.

The young surveyor, George Washington, was named to command the Virginia Regiment and immediately wrote: 'As His Majesty is pleased to make me a military officer, please send for Scott, my tailor, to make me a proper suit of regimentals to be here by His Majesty's Birthday. I do not much like gaiety in dress, but I conceive this necessary. I do not much care for lace on a coat, but a neat embroidered button hole . . . a good laced hat and two pairs of stockings, one silk and one fine thread.' His officers were ordered in 1755 to have uniforms of 'fine blue broadcloth faced and cuffed with scarlet and trimmed with silver lace. The waistcoat scarlet with plain silver lace (if to be had.) The breeches to be blue and everyone to provide himself with a silver laced hat of a fashionable size.'

While the officers had rather spiffy uniforms, a regular officer wrote in his journal that: 'The Privates are a poor mean ragged set of men . . . their officers are sober modest men and such as have upon service express themselves very distinctly and sensibly. They make a decent appearance, being clothed in blue faced with scarlet, gilt buttons, laced waistcoats and hats but the ordinary soldiers have no uniforms nor do they effect any regularity.'

This state of affairs was not of Washington's doing. In 1754 he wrote to Virginia's governor: 'I again take the liberty of reminding your Honour of the great necessity there is of a regulation in the soldiers pay and that a deduction be made for the country to furnish them with cloathes, otherwise they never will be fit for service, they are now naked and cannot get credit even for hatts and are teasing the officers every day to furnish them with these and other necessaries.' Later he wrote again,

'We daily experience the great necessity for cloathing the men, as we find the generality of those, who are to be enlisted, are of those loose idle persons that are quite destitute of House and Home and, I may truely say, many of them of Cloaths . . . there is many of them without Shoes, others want Stockings, some are without Shirts and not a few that have scarce a Coat or waistcoat to their backs . . . I really believe every man of them, for their own credits sake, is willing to be Cloathed at their own expense.'

The governor agreed and had money deducted from the men's pay 'to purchase a Coat and Breeches of red Cloth'. So it was that that year a deserter from the regiment wore 'a red Coat turn'd up with blue', while three others simply had 'red Coats'. The last three also had leather breeches.

Officers were then ordered to obtain a 'common soldiers Dress, for Detachments and Duty in the Woods'.

Regardless of dress or numbers, the provincials were simply not of regular quality in discipline or fighting abilities. It was on the regulars' shoulders that the bulk of fighting fell.

And it fell hard. Duty in the American wilderness was dull to the men, wearing on uniform and equipment, and damaging to regimental unity and discipline. Even though at the end the British had won, they won at a tremendous cost to the Army. An inspection report on the 15th Regiment, which had seen much American service, shortly after the war's end is probably typical of the vast majority of units then:

'Officers – Armed with Fuzees. Uniforms old, but good – Red, faced and lapelled with Yellow, Silver Lace, Red Waistcoats, and White Breeches

N.C.O.'s – Made a good appearance, the Serjeants had no Sashes

Men – In general very low, and many of them old

Exercise – Tolerably well, but in slow time

Firings – Having no powder they could only go through the motions, but performed the platoon exercise with tolerable exactness.

Marching – Not well

Arms – Very bad

Accoutrements – Old, but in pretty good repair

Clothing – Good

Considering this Regiment's long service in America, and having been situated in a Country where only a small part of the year could be appropriated to the Discipline of the Men, they made a better appearance than could be expected.

It was a good army. It had done valuable service, and now it needed rest and rebuilding.'

# 3

# The British Army 1764–1783

The first thing the Army would need would be new uniforms. Not only were their old ones worn out, but, more important, they were horribly out of style.

Therefore, in 1768, an entirely new uniform Royal Warrant was issued, which made sweeping changes in the Regular Army's dress. Other, equally major, changes were made, not because of the Royal Warrant, but simply because of changes in clothing style.

The hat changed from the tricorne of three equal sides to more of a bicorne with a flat back and the front cock pointed up in the air, instead of being level with the ground like the other two cocks. It was still bound up in white tape for battalion infantrymen, often with a tassel hanging from the right side for decoration. A black cockade and regimental button were worn on the left side. The whole hat was worn with the front cock over the left eye, so it would not get in the musket's way while the soldier was drilling.

When the Army returned to America for its next war, small hats with the narrow brims simply cocked up on the left side, were widely issued. These were usually, but not always, bound up with white tape, and had the cockade and regimental button worn on the turned-up brim.

Officers often bound up their hats in gold or silver,

*This private in a battalion company of the 64th Regiment of Foot shows the classic British soldier following the Royal Warrant of 1768 – the small round cuffs, the long, thin lapels, and white small clothes. In America, conditions would cause modifications to this perfect example of the regulation uniform.* (Embleton/Osprey)

depending on their regiment, although many officers preferred plain hats.

Shirts remained the same, but stocks were now black. Each man was to receive two stocks, one of velvet worn for dress, and one of horse-hair for duty.

Waistcoats were now 'to be plain, without either Embroidery or Lace'. They were also now white wool, as were the breeches. Some waistcoats were made with pocket-flaps; others, in the more modern style, without.

*The basic uniform, following the Royal Warrant of 1768, is worn by this man of the 'Highland Company' of the 25th Regiment of Foot. Because of the different, light infantry nature of his company, his coat is cut shorter than usual, and his cap is more like that of light infantry. (Reproduced by gracious permission of H.M. The Queen)*

*Coat of the 101st Regiment of Foot, which served between 1781 and 1785. The coat has 'winged lappets', connecting lapels and collar, an unusual feature among regular British coats, and a functioning set of buttons on the cuff edge. Note the pockets inside the skirts. As they were serving in India, the coat's lining has probably been removed because of the heat. (National Army Museum)*

Gaiters were to be of black linen, instead of white or brown. According to the regulations of the 37th Regiment of Foot in 1774: 'Linen gaiters to be regimental on every occasion except upon a march, when those made of black cloth (i.e. wool) with round black horn buttons are to be worn.' While gaiters were still the over-the-knee type, short gaiters, just reaching to the calf were allowed for duty, and in the 37th these were made '. . . according to Regimental form and have 9 buttons'. In addition: 'Plain white stockings to be constantly worn with short gaiters.' The long gaiters were also described for the 37th. 'The tongue of the gaiter must cover the shoe buckle, the tops are to be lined with white edged with red, the garters of an inch breadth upon them and to buckle behind, over the seam of the gaiter. . . .'

The coat itself was in for quite a number of alterations. Sleeves were made tighter and longer, with small round cuffs and four buttons and a piece of regimental lace sewn around each buttonhole on them. The collar was now a turn-down, wide affair, pointed in the back, which buttoned on top of the lapels. The lapels now became narrower, only some three inches wide, and longer, ending below or level with the waistcoat's bottom edge.

Each lapel had ten buttons on it, the top button also buttoning into the collar and a piece of lace sewn around each buttonhole. These pieces of lace were put down in rectangles or in 'bastions', five-pointed shapes. Lace was also sewn around the four buttons on the coat's two outside, false pockets. The coat's real pocket was sewn inside the coat-skirts. Linings were now white wool, not the facing colour, for the whole Army.

In America, in the field, many men seemed to have worn short, plain, red tail-less jackets as much as, if not more than, regulation long coats. These may have been sleeved red waistcoats, or cut-down long coats, if not made new in America.

Buttons, which had been plain pewter or brass, were now marked with the regimental number like French ones. These were quite plain in regiments like the 10th Regiment, where the colonel was loth to waste money on fancy extras for his men, or quite ornate. The 42nd's buttons had a wreath of thistles and roses, a crown, and the regimental number. Regimental buttons were used on waistcoats, too, although probably not on breeches, haversacks or anything not for show.

Corporals were marked by a white silk epaulette or aiguellette worn on the right shoulder. A sergeant wore silver lace on his hat and plain, not regimental, white lace on his coat. In addition, he wore a scarlet worsted sash with a stripe the colour of his facings through the middle. Infantry sergeants knotted their sashes, which were worn under their coats, on the left side.

Swords were no longer to be issued to anybody but sergeants, grenadiers, and musicians. Sergeants wore their swords on buff waistbelts worn under their waistcoats.

Other ranks also wore their waistbelts under their coats. These were still made of buff leather, whitened, and considerably narrower than those worn in the last war. They were usually still made with frogs for two weapons, but only the bayonet was carried. Later, waistbelts with only one frog were issued.

During the American War of Independence men began adopting the practice of wearing their waistbelts over their shoulders, and many belts were

*An officer of the 4th Regiment of Foot, by Gainsborough, c. 1770. He wears his sword suspended from a whitened buff belt worn outside his coat, with a silver belt-plate. Note the black garter belts used to hold up the bulky stockings, showing under the breeches.* (National Gallery of Victoria)

actually cut up and restitched so that this could be easily done. When that happened, the frame brass buckle which had been worn began to be replaced by one of sheet brass, usually engraved with the regimental number.

In addition, soldiers were wont to put a strip of red cloth on their coats' left shoulders to keep the cartridge-box sling in place. When the bayonet-belt began to be worn over the other shoulder, another shoulder-strap was added there, too. By 1782–3 some regiments began wearing shoulder-straps made of the facing colour and bound with regimental lace. When the soldiers took off their accoutrements, however, they rarely rebuttoned their shoulder-straps, much to the officers' dismay.

Officers, too, began to use belts worn over the shoulder to carry their swords. These, too, were generally whitened buff leather, usually made with an oval silver or gold plate bearing the regiment's number and badges. These belts were kept down under the officer's single epaulette which was worn on the right shoulder regardless of rank. It was, in

*A British officer's standard sword, used throughout the period, now in the City of Lancaster Museum.* (Peter W. Joslin)

*As in the previous war, the sergeant's rank is indicated by his plain white lace and crimson sash with its facing colour. This sergeant of the 29th Regiment of Foot is dressed perfectly according to regulation.* (Embleton/Osprey)

British generals had two regulation coats, ordered in 1767, one
heavily laced in gold for state occasions, and a plainer scarlet
'frock' with blue facings and some gold embroidery. This
major-general, as most general officers in the field, wears
his 'frock' in the latest fashion, with the lapels buttoned across
his chest. Buttonholes were set in pairs for major-generals
and threes for lieutenant-generals, but there was no uniformity
in epaulettes. Plain frock-coats, lacking any gold like that
worn by General Wolfe in the previous war, were authorized in
1786. (Embleton/Osprey)

As with the last war, two colours, the King's Colour and the
Regimental Colour, were carried by ensigns. This young
officer carries the somewhat battle-torn Regimental Colour of the
55th Regiment of Foot. (Embleton/Osprey)

fact, impossible to tell from the epaulette what the officer's rank was. In such a small, professional army, it was considered enough that most officers would know each other, while the other ranks would quickly learn to know their own officers and would salute all officers, anyway.

As officers moved their sword-belts outside their coats, their crimson silk net sashes were now moved in and wrapped around the waist. Foot officers, like sergeants, knotted theirs on the left, while mounted unit officers knotted theirs on the right. The sash was still quite wide and said to be capable of use as a stretcher to carry its wounded owner from the field.

Officers' coats were the same as other ranks, although made of better dyed cloth and therefore true scarlet, while the other ranks' coats appeared more of a dull, dark brick red. According to the 37th's regulations: 'The utmost exactness and nicety is required in the making up of the Regimentals, in the pattern of the epaulettes, the breadth of the lace, and in the distance from and length of the buttonhole. The King's regulations to be strictly attended to in the breadth of the lapels and cuffs, the skirt ornaments to be perfectly uniform.'

Most rank-and-file coats seem to have had no ornaments where their coat-tails hooked together. Officers, on the other hand, used hearts, sometimes of brass which were often engraved, and sometimes of facing colour wool. Other shapes, such as diamonds, were also used. Some other ranks may have used loops of lace as skirt turnback ornaments.

Besides the fancier turnbacks, officers often had their coats embroidered with metallic thread where the men had lace. At times woven metallic lace was used. In some regiments, such as the 40th, 47th, and 62nd, the officers had perfectly plain lapels, cuffs, and pockets. The 55th's officers, on the other hand, had 'button holes looped with narrow gold lace', while those of the 63rd had 'silver embroidered buttonholes'. Buttons in most cases were similar to those of the men but silver- or gold-plated.

Not all the buttons in a regiment worn at the same time were necessarily the same design. Besides the elaborate 42nd button, the men also wore buttons with a plain number 42 and 'French' scroll and dot, and others simply with a plain number.

Officers were also distinguished by their gorgets,

gold or white, with the King's coat of arms engraved on them. These were worn on duty – in the 37th they were 'to be tied with yellow ribbon' – around the neck. Usually, in America, they were among the first things discarded when the fighting started.

The spontoon was the officer's weapon, although, again, in America, it was rarely used. Officers much preferred to carry fusils – lighter and better-made copies of the Brown Bess. The officer's other weapon, the sword, had a sword-knot with a wide scarlet stripe and several narrow gold stripes woven into it. According to the 37th's orders 'None but the Regimental Swords were to be worn,' and 'those at all times'.

In horse regiments each officer and man also had a brace of pin-fastened, brass-mounted pistols, carried in holsters worn on either side of the saddle.

The sweeping changes in dress affected not only the English foot and mounted troops, but those of Scotland, too. There was only one Highland regiment, the 42nd, left in 1775, but the Highlanders had done such a good job in the last war that it was certain that when the problem of putting down the rebellion got out of hand, Highland regiments would be raised again. The first to be raised bore a famous name from the last war, Fraser's Highlanders, the 71st Regiment now, still with white facings.

In rapid succession, then, came McLeod's Highlanders (the 73rd) with green facings, the Argyll Highlanders (the 74th) with yellow facings, MacDonell's Highlanders (the 76th) with deep green facings, the Seaforth Highlanders (the 78th) with yellowish buff facings, and the Aberdeen Highlanders (the 81st) with white facings. Another regiment, the Athol Highlanders (the 77th) was raised but mutinied at the prospect of being sent to America and was quickly disbanded.

Other than the facings, Highland regimental dress conformed largely to that of the 42nd. The coats were short, but they now had the small round cuff and long lapels with an overlapping collar of English coats. While Lowland and English regimental coats were made with lapels which buttoned across the chest for warmth, the Highland coat was made with sewn-down lapels. The fly plaid was considered enough to provide warmth.

Waistcoats were now white. The kilt and separate fly plaid, of the government sett, were worn by all

Highland regiments. Stockings were still almost knee length, red and white checked.

A sporran, usually a simple natural-coloured leather thing, was worn in front of the kilt, quite high and touching the waistcoat. The 42nd's colonel purchased fancy decorated goatskin sporrans for dress wear in 1769, but these were rarely worn.

The cartridge-box was still the small plain box worn on the waistbelt, along with the bayonet scabbard. Upon reaching America in 1775 the 42nd's men chose to leave their broadswords, which they no longer used in combat, aboard their ship, and with them went their sword-belts. Their metal pistols were also left behind, and most of them carried no dirks. Like the rest of the Army, Highlanders carried no weapons other than their Brown Besses and bayonets.

Their bonnets had changed, too. They were now rather tall, with bands of woven worsted tape forming a chequered pattern of red and white; red, white, and green; or red, white, and blue, depending on the maker. The bonnet itself was still blue. It had a heavy leather stiffener inside for protection against sword blows. A red tourie was in the centre of the top, and a small piece of bearskin was worn from the cockade and regimental button or badge on the left to the tourie. The men generally liked their bonnets fancier than issued and bought black feathers for them themselves.

Highland officers were allowed to wear epaulettes on both shoulders, and often still carried dirks and pistols, as well as their broadswords.

Highlanders carried the same tin waterbottles as the rest of the Army. All the men carried natural-coloured linen haversacks, closed with three plain pewter buttons. Knapsacks were originally the same over-the-shoulder types as used in the previous war. During the period, however, they were slowly changed to a type worn square on the back, with a sling around each arm and a crossbelt buckled across the chest. When a blanket was carried it was often worn as a rolled-up blanket roll, slung from the right shoulder to the left side and underneath the knapsack and its straps. The knapsack's straps were quite compressing, especially considering all the rest of the accoutrements worn across the chest, and soldiers often marched with their cross-strap unbuckled.

A soldier was to carry his 'necessaries' in his knapsack. According to a military guide of the period, these were to include

'three shirts; two white stocks (or rollers); one black hair stock; one pair of brass clasps for ditto; three pair of white yarn stockings; two pair of linen socks, dipped in oil, to be worn on a march, under spatterdashes, when necessary; two pair of long linen gaiters, if belonging to the guards; one pair of black long gaiters, with black tops for ditto; one pair of half spatterdashes; one pair of linen drawers; one pair of red skirt breeches; one red cap; one cockade; one knapsack; one haversack; one pair of shoe buckles; one pair of garter-buckles; black leather garters; two pair of shoes; one oil bottle; one brush and picker; one worm; one turn-key; one hammer-cap, and one stopper.'

Again, quite a load for the poor soldier to carry.

Added to that was the black leather cartridge-box, now to hold thirty-six rounds of heavy 0·75-calibre ammunition. The box now had only two buckles on the sling, having eliminated the one on the centre of the chest. The box's flap was often decorated with a brass badge, often a circle with the regimental number or Royal Cypher with a crown on top, backed up with a piece of red wool. The 'brush and picker' was usually attached to the cartridge-box sling.

The Brown Bess itself had changed somewhat since the last war. In 1768, as with uniforms, a new model, the Short Land Model, was officially ordered. Its overall appearance had changed little, but the barrel was now only forty-two inches long. The top ramrod-pipe had been enlarged to enable one to return the ramrod more quickly. The side-plate had been flattened and simplified. The whole musket was slimmer and lighter than the old model had been. The bayonet remained the same.

The musket's sling was white, except for the Highlanders who had black, and pioneers who had no slings at all. The pioneers' job was to clear the regiment's way in battle or on the march, and to do such they were equipped with axes and saws. Furthermore, to keep their clothes clean, they were given natural-coloured leather aprons which covered almost their whole bodies. Their accoutrements were carried on belts, the saw in a leather case suspended from a crossbelt worn from the right shoulder to the left side, with the saw in a case on the same belt on the middle of the back. They carried their axes in their hands, over one shoulder. Pioneers of the 27th Regiment of Foot wore grenadier swords and this practice may have been widespread.

In the Royal Warrant they were ordered to wear 'a Cap with a Leather Crown, and a Black Bearskin Front, on which is to be the King's Crest in White, on a Red Ground; also an Axe and Saw. The Number of the Regiment to be on the back Part of the Cap.' The cap was made with a red bag inside the cap's centre, surrounded with black bearskin, and a grenade stamped with the regimental number in the rear of the back. White cords were

*This officer of the 42nd has acquired a uniform which conforms to his regiment's changes made by the 1768 Warrant. Highland officers were allowed two epaulettes.* (Embleton/Osprey)

*After some years in the field, men of the 42nd had little more than their bonnets and short coats to show their Highland origins. Gaiter trousers were made from old tents; tomahawks replaced broadswords. The rest of the kit was the same as worn by Lowlanders and Englishmen.* (Embleton/Osprey)

worn along the edge of the bag and bearskin, with a tassel hanging off the right side. The cap was, in fact, quite similar to those worn by another separate group within the regiment – the grenadiers.

The grenadier company was still the same sort of company as it had been. When war came to America again in 1775, the grenadier companies were taken from their regiments and put into separate battalions. Thus the 1st and 2nd Grenadier Battalions were created to serve in America. The men during this service wore their regular regimental uniform.

The grenadier's uniform also had been changed

*This interesting picture of a 42nd flank company officer is closely based on a contemporary portrait. He wears gold wings, and a regular set of infantry gaiters with leather tops. He has kept his broadsword, sash, and gorget. (Embleton/Osprey)*

*According to the 1768 Warrant, musicians in regiments with white or buff facings had red waistcoats and breeches, with coats of facing colours. This drummer of the 31st Regiment of Foot is so dressed, with a coat laced 'as the Colonel shall think fit'. He has the white goatskin knapsack on his back. (Embleton/Osprey)*

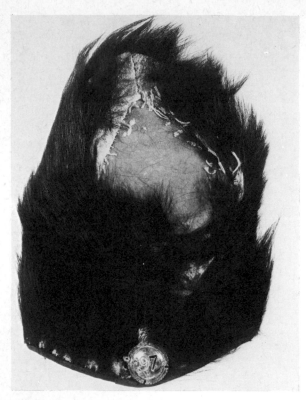

*Back view of the grenadier's cap. A white metal 'flaming grenade' has the regimental number stamped into it. The wool bag showing at the centre of the cap is red, supposedly plush, but often wool.* (National Army Museum)

by the 1768 Warrant. His coat was made the same as the rest of the regiment's, but it now had 'the usual Round Wings of Red Cloth, on the Point of the Shoulder, with Six Loops of the same Sort of Lace as on the Button holes and a Border round the Bottom (of the wing).' Matchcases were still worn on cartridge-box slings.

The grenadier's crowning glory was, as in the previous war, his cap. The wool embroidered cap had been discarded, as in the French Army earlier, in favour of black bearskin caps, taller in front than behind, with a red wool bag. The bag was to have been made of plush, but often last year's coats were used. White cords similar to those in the pioneer's cap were worn. On front there was a tin plate, with a japanned black background, bearing the Royal Cypher, crown, a knight's helmet, and the motto, *Nec Asper Terrent*. On the back's centre was a white metal flaming grenade with the regimental number on it. Even though this fancy plate was strictly

regulation by the Royal Warrant, in this case the Warrant was ignored by some regiments – as in fact all aspects of the Warrant were ignored in one way or another by virtually every regiment in the Army. The 25th Regiment of Foot had perfectly plain bearskin caps without any front-plate at all.

Officially in the previous war, the grenadier company and the battalion companies made up the whole regiment. The importance of light infantry was that war's major lesson, however, and it had been learned. Now each regiment had one company assigned as its light company, in orders dated 1770.

In 1774 seven light companies, drawn from various regiments, were made into a temporary light battalion at Salisbury where they learned a new set

*The drummer's regulation cap was quite like the grenadier's cap, only slightly shorter and the front bore the design of drums, crossed fifes, and other musical instruments. The same type of stamped tin plate, with a japanned black background, was used on grenadiers' caps.* (National Army Museum)

of light infantry manœuvres written by General Howe. This practice was vital for the new light infantrymen, because the new company was usually resisted by the regimental colonels. The light companies looked different from the rest of the regiment on parade. Since they were to be detached from the regiment in the field, colonels took advantage of them to fill their ranks with the worst soldiers in the regiment.

Light company men were to be trained in 'leaping, running, climbing precipices, swimming, skirmishing through woods, loading and firing in different positions at marks, and marching with great

*The small visor can be turned down or up to shade the eyes on this leather cap, quite likely a period light infantry cap.* (National Army Museum)

*A private in the 13th Regiment's picket company wears another variation of the light infantry cap.* (Reproduced by gracious permission of H.M. The Queen)

*The first light companies, following their disbanding in 1763, were called 'picket companies'. This private is in the picket company of the 11th Regiment of Foot.* (Reproduced by gracious permission of H.M. The Queen)

*Two black lines were added to the regimental lace of the 47th Regiment of Foot, in mourning for General Wolfe. This grenadier corporal wears the new lace on his uniform, along with his rank-knot worn on the right shoulder. (Embleton/Osprey)*

*According to a contemporary painting, apparently done for an eyewitness, light infantry at the battle of Germantown wore short, all-red jackets, white gaiter trousers, and 'slouched' hats, probably with an animal tail as decoration. The light infantryman seems to have exchanged his small issue cartridge-box for a captured Continental one. (Embleton/Osprey)*

Even officers, such as this one of the 5th Regiment of Foot, simplified their uniforms in the field considerably. Again based in part on the painting of the battle of Germantown, this officer wears an uncocked hat with feathers and a sword to suit himself. (Embleton/Osprey)

During the Burgoyne campaign all regiments were ordered to cut their coats short and convert their cocked hats into caps, to make the entire Army look like light infantry. This private of the 62nd Regiment of Foot has also sewn down his coat's false pocket vertically, like those of Highland regiments, and shortened it to only three, instead of the normal four, buttonholes. (Embleton/Osprey)

Ein Britischer Soldat auf dem Posten, in der Canadischen Winter Kleidung. 1766.

*An eyewitness to the Burgoyne expedition sketched this British soldier in winter dress in Canada c. 1778, not 1766 as noted. His coat appears to have been made from an issue blanket, and his cap probably from an old regimental coat and bound around with fur.* (New York Public Library)

rapidity'. This type of active campaigning would be difficult to do with the long coats and tricornes of the battalion men, or grenadiers' bearskins. A new dress was required.

The original idea was to keep the company in the same dress as the rest of the battalion. When it would be called out as light infantry, the uniform could be easily converted to the light one. This way the regiment would look good on parade, yet light infantry uniforms could be made when needed.

Converting the old uniforms consisted of turning the long coat into a short jacket by cutting off the tails; of making cut-down caps from tricornes by cutting off the brims, and changing the cartridge-boxes from over-the-shoulder to being worn on a waistbelt. This may have been the most economical way to come up with a light dress, but it would not make the best uniforms possible. Special uniforms were ordered for the light infantrymen. In 1770 it was ordered that they should wear black leather caps, made with a piece of iron plate on top and

three chains wrapped around the cap's crown and a turned-up flap in front bearing a painted crown, GR, and the regimental number. Most of these seem to have had the letters LI painted on them, too, but this was ordered to be done away with in 1771.

In addition, waistcoats were to be red, not white, and some regiments, such as the 5th Regiment of

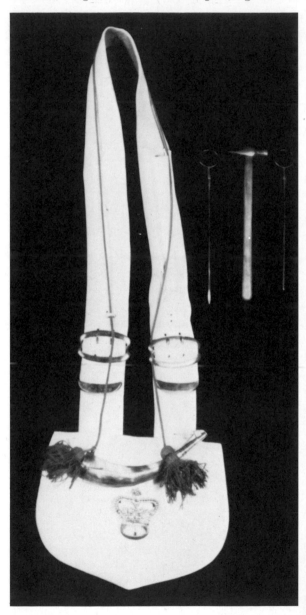

*An artilleryman's cartridge-pouch of whitened buff leather, with priming-horn attached on red cords and the gunner's vent-picks and hammer.* (National Army Museum)

Foot, decorated them with regimental lace, which was officially ordered in 1771. Breeches were left white or buff, depending on regimental practice, and half-gaiters instead of full gaiters were always to be worn. In 1771, as well, it was ordered that the men were to have 'a small cartridge box to contain nine rounds in one row, to be worn before, with a belt of tanned leather round the waist. The belt to be furnished with two frogs, one for the bayonet, the other for the hatchet occasionally, which at other times will be tyed upon the knapsack.' One box similar to this description, which was captured after the battle of Lexington and Concord, has a gold embossed crown and GR on its front flap.

While most regiments made some attempt generally to follow regulations, combat practices in America caused some changes to be adopted. The small, nine-round cartridge-box, for example, was totally inadequate to hold enough ammunition. One British officer, after the battle of Brandywine, noted that 'The Light Infy Accoutrements . . . [were] mostly Rebel.' The average Continental pouch, with a light linen sling but holding some twenty-four rounds was by far superior to the nine-hole box and more than enough were captured to equip all the light infantry in America.

caps bearing an allegorical scene, a bugle horn and the words, 'Light Infantry'. The 13th had a cap turned up back and front with a fox's brush sticking out of each side. The 69th had both a front plate and visor, with a red horse-hair plume and a turned-up back, probably used as a rain protector.

Uniform or not, it hardly mattered to the colonels, because their light companies, as their grenadiers, were taken from the regiments when they arrived in America and made the 1st and 2nd Light Battalions.

To make up for the loss of these two companies, and to help increase the Army's size during the war, two more battalion companies per regiment were authorized. Each regiment of foot would now contain a colonel, a lieutenant-colonel, a major, nine captains, fourteen lieutenants, ten ensigns, one chaplain, an adjutant, a quartermaster, a surgeon and his mate, thirty-six sergeants, thirty-six corporals, twenty-four drummers, two fifers, and 672 privates, giving it 811 men all told. These included three 'contingent' men per company, as there had been in the last war – non-existent men whose pay went to widows, fancier uniforms, or whatever the officers wished. In actual service each company generally mustered some twenty-five men.

*An officer's shoulder-belt plate of the 4th Battalion, Royal Regiment of Artillery, which served in America.*

*The badge worn, backed up by red, on the Royal Artillery cartridge-pouch.* (Charleston, S.C., Museum)

While tan leather was ordered for belts, dozens of inspection reports criticize various light companies for having buff or black leather crossbelts.

Caps were another major area of variation. The 4th (King's Own), for example, in 1774 had tricornes bound with scalloped lace, while the 5th had

The Royal Regiment of Artillery was organized differently. It was made up of four battalions, each with ten companies. Unlike the last war where artillery played a fairly minor role, artillery in this war would be rather important and the whole 4th Battalion was sent to America.

Artillerymen still wore blue-faced red coats, although the cut had been changed to conform to the rest of the Army. Their lace was plain yellow. White waistcoats, stocks, and breeches were uniform. Men of the 4th Battalion decorated their tricornes with a black feather stuck in the cockade as sort of a battalion badge.

Officers used swords instead of fusils and they wore their sashes around their waists. In the field they wore plain, unlaced blue frocks, while the men wore blue jackets and brown trousers. White buff

*Thomas Boothby Parkyns, 15th Light Dragoons, wears the typical light dragoon uniform of the period.* (National Army Museum)

*Dress of the Royal Regiment of Artillery was modified to conform to the design of the rest of the Army. This officer wears its regulation uniform, but no fusil or pouch which they were ordered to discard about 1770.* (Embleton/Osprey)

cartridge-boxes and white buff belts with frogs for a hanger and a bayonet, were worn across their chests.

As the war in America increased in size, the 4th was reinforced by six companies of the 3rd Battalion and two of the 1st Battalion. Some seventy men of the Royal Irish Artillery were sent as reinforcements, in identical uniforms to the Royal Artillery, in 1777.

Another organization sent in small groups to America was that of the Brigade of Guards. The Brigade was made up of the 1st Foot Guards, with three battalions of twenty-eight companies; the Coldstream Guards, with two battalions of eighteen companies; and the 3rd Foot Guards, with two battalions of eighteen companies. The Guards were a superior organization, and their ranks were higher than those of the rest of the Army. All their field officers were at least brevet-colonels, often generals, while the captains and captain-lieutenants were lieutenant-colonels in the Army. Even their lieutenants were listed as captains in the Army. Only the ensigns were carried as ensigns on the *Army Lists.*

When the time came to send a battalion of Guardsmen to America, it was made up of ten companies, four from the 1st Foot Guards and three each from the other two regiments. Edward Mathew, commanding the battalion, was a Guards captain, both a lieutenant-colonel and brevet-colonel in the Army, and a local brigadier-general in America. Only those captains who were not brevet-colonels were allowed to command the companies in America.

A composite grenadier company was sent from all

three battalions, while the first three companies of the 1st, along with their headquarters (then called the Brigade Company), and the 1st and 2nd companies of the Coldstreamers and the 3rd, made up the battalion.

Guardsmen's uniforms were similar to the rest of the Army, all with blue facings, save that the lace was plain white and the coats were much more elaborately laced.

As the war in America was large enough, and fought in a sufficiently European manner to require artillery and Guardsmen, it also required dragoons. The first regiment sent to America was the 17th Regiment of Light Dragoons, with white facings, followed by the 16th Regiment of Light Dragoons, with blue facings. Dress of the mounted men was similar to that of foot, although boots were generally worn. Officers' and sergeants' sashes were knotted on the right, and brass or leather helmets, decorated with horse-hair plumes, were worn.

Once in the field, it would appear that the 17th put their red coats aside and wore all-green coats, although they kept their brass helmets, with the red crests and turbans. The cap fronts were trimmed in black fur and bore the regiment's 'skull and cross-bones' badge.

Their arms, wrote a dragoon captain in 1778, consisted of

'Carbines about 2 Feet 5 Inches Long in the Barrels (with or without a Bayonet about 1 Foot Long in the Blade,) and a Pair of Pistols 9 Inches long in the Barrels, and a Sword about 37 Inches long in the Blade, either crooked or straight according to the Regulations of the Regiment, in a Belt worn over the Right shoulder (General Burgoyme's Regiment [the 16th] carry them on a Waist-Belt, as they use a small Black Leather Pouch on their Left Sides, fastened to a Belt which goes over the Right Shoulder).'

The 16th, also, did not seem to have carried bayonets in America.

The war was rough on dragoons and, in 1778, the 16th was so depleted that its few remaining men were transferred to the 17th and the officers returned home to recruit. The 17th lasted in America throughout the war.

Such long service should be rewarded and some regiments did make provisions for such rewards.

*Facings of the 16th (Queen's) Regiment of Light Dragoons were changed from black to blue in 1766. Officers and sergeants in the regiment had white lace, while corporals had a narrow silver edge around their coat cuffs. (Embleton/Osprey)*

*A light dragoon's typical brass helmet, with horsehair crest and metallic thread tassels hanging behind.* (National Army Museum)

After the end of the previous war the Colonel of the 5th Regiment of Foot founded a regimental order of merit for other ranks, consisting of three classes. Those with seven years' service wore a bronze medal; those with fourteen, a silver one; and those with twenty-one years a green ribbon with the word 'merit' in gold letters worn on their left breast. Such awards were strictly regimental, and not army-wide.

Probably an easier way to see that a soldier had spent some years in America was his patched and worn dress and, in a smooth-shaven army, his beard. When the 42nd finally left New York for Halifax in 1783 one of its soldiers recorded in his diary: 'Them among us who have grown hair upon the face of our countinence some very much and others a little bit, have been told to get it shaved off good and well for the review which we are preparing for now. Ensign Campbell says that runners [sideburns] will be overlooked but no full-haired faced will be passed. Top lips to be shaved to and all.'

More important orders than those concerning shaving, at least for the future Army, were received by most regiments in August, 1782. Those received by the 19th Regiment of Foot are typical of them all:

'His Majesty having been pleased to order the

19th Regiment of Foot which you command should take the County name of the 19th or 1st York North Riding Regiment and be looked upon as attached to that Division of the Country, I am to acquaint you that it is His Majesty's further Pleasure that you should in all things conform to that Idea and endeavour by all means in your power to cultivate and improve the connection so as to create attachment between the County and the Regiment which may at all Times be useful towards recruiting the Regiment . . . and by prescribing the greatest diligence towards your officers and recruiting parties, and by suitable attention to the Gentlemen and considerable inhabitants. . . .'

Of all changes in the Army's organization during the American War of Independence this is probably the most important one. It set up the connection between each shire and regiment which, in many cases, has endured to this day.

This may have been the most important long-range order of the entire period, but the Army's immediate problem was winning the war, and that was quite a difficult one. Not only were there rebellious subjects to deal with, but they had been joined by regulars from France and Spain, and other countries were beginning to pick away at the British Empire. The Regular Army itself would be unable to handle the entire problem.

# 4

# Germans and Provincials 1775–1783

As it had done in the past, the British government decided to hire regular soldiers from other countries. It turned first to Russia, which, between wars itself, was not interested in supplying troops. Nor was Prussia, but some of the small German states whose main business was supplying soldiers for hire, were.

Contracts were quickly drawn up whereby, eventually, Hesse-Cassel supplied nineteen infantry regiments with necessary artillery; Hesse-Hanau, one infantry regiment and an artillery company; Anspach-Beyreuth, two infantry regiments with artillery; Brunswick, five infantry regiments, a grenadier battalion, a dragoon regiment and artillery; and Anhalt-Zerbst, an infantry regiment and supporting troops. Waldeck, whose two infantry regiments were already in the Dutch service, raised a third regiment specifically for the British service. Hanover supplied three regiments to the Gibraltar garrison, two to Minorca, and two to India. Individuals from Hanover were also recruited to serve in regular British regiments.

The typical German infantry regiment was made up of a lieutenant-colonel, a major, twenty-five officers, including five non-combatant officers such as the surgeon, sixty N.C.O.s, twenty-two musicians, and 525 rank and file. As with most units then, there were generally fewer men actually serving in any given regiment than there should have been. Each regiment had both a grenadier company and battalion companies. The grenadiers usually served with their own regiments, however, to conform to British practices, being put into grenadier battalions when the regiments reached America. Regiments from Hesse-Hanau and Brunswick had light infantry companies, called 'chasseurs', as well.

In the other states the type of work done by light infantrymen was done by the *Feldjägers*. These were men recruited from the forests, used to hunting, and armed with short, European rifles, firing large balls. As the rifles were made by individual gunsmiths, not according to set patterns, they differed in detail. Generally, however, they were three feet ten inches long, with a wooden patch-box, pin-fastened, and made with brass furniture. The rifles took no bayonet so the Jägers carried short, straight-bladed hunting-swords.

Oddly, for men whose main duty would be in woods, their cocked hats had brims cut much larger than those of battalion men. Otherwise, the Jägers were rather sensibly dressed in dark green coats. Facings and linings were red, although those of Hesse-Cassel were crimson, while those of Brunswick were plain red with green linings. Details such as waistcoat, breeches, and gaiter colour would also differ from state to state. Their sergeants had gold lace on their cuffs and a white feather topped red on their hats, while officers had gold lace both on lapels and cuffs and a plain white feather.

Both mounted and foot Jäger units were used in America, both originally wearing tall boots. Boots were pretty uncomfortable to wear when on foot in America, and most foot Jägers switched to long brown or grey linen gaiters and often to gaitered trousers made from old tents.

The Jäger coat was cut similar to all German coats, which were largely based on those worn in the Prussian Army. German coats were made of coarse, heavy blue wool, lined with a slightly lighter-weight red wool. Buttons were plain brass or pewter. As with British coats, the wool was heavy enough for the coats to be unhemmed. They were usually made without collars, the cuffs, the single shoulder-strap on the left shoulder, and the lapels being made of a facing colour cloth – red, yellow, white, black, or orange. Garrison regiments, of which Hesse-Cassel sent four, had no lapels but small, turn-down collars of the facing colour. Collars were also used by some regular regiments, as well, and exact cuff designs differed from state to state, and from regiment to regiment. Wool lace, sometimes plain and sometimes with a woven design, was used by some but not all regiments.

An important feature of the German coat was the shortness of the sleeves, which exposed a great deal of shirtsleeve. Frederick of Prussia thought such short sleeves made his men look taller.

*The magnificent uniform worn by men of the Anhalt-Zerbst Infantry Regiment was largely inspired by those of the Austrian Army. In the field a tricorne replaced the felt shako, while linen gaitered trousers replaced breeches and boots, and possibly white linen waistcoats were worn instead of red woollen ones. (Embleton/Osprey)*

*Three companies of Anspach Jägers were attached to the Hesse-Cassel Field Jäger Corps, although their green linings were different from the Hessian crimson ones. This private has obtained a pair of Hessian green breeches to wear instead of his issue white ones. After Yorktown all Anspachers were posted to their Field Jäger Battalion. (Embleton/Osprey)*

The shirt was white linen, made without a collar. The black or red stock, depending on the regiment, had a white strip along its top to look like the top of a shirt collar. Waistcoats and breeches were of white or pale yellow wool, again depending on the regiment, with the breeches tied at the bottom rather than buckled or buttoned like British ones. In the field in Canada, Germans cut up old tents and made

*The entire corps of artillery of Hesse-Cassel was hired by the British government, and fought in America. The uniform was similar to most artillerymen's, save that the facings were more crimson than scarlet and waistcoat and breeches were a yellowish-buff colour. (Embleton/Osprey)*

*The only German dragoon regiment sent to America was the Brunswick Dragoon Regiment Prinz Ludwig Ernst. Sent without horses, the men traded their long boots for gaiters and fought on foot. (Embleton/Osprey)*

long gaitered trousers which were more comfortable than breeches. In the winter in New York both Germans and British received similar gaitered trousers made of blue, green, red, and brown wool. Otherwise, thigh-length black linen gaiters, fastened with plain brass buttons, were worn over shoes, stockings, and breeches.

Sergeants had their uniforms laced with silver, and carried halberds. Spontoons, much like British ones but elaborately engraved, were carried by officers. Officers were also set apart by their large, ornate gorgets, often enamelled with different colours, worn usually under their coats. Officers had sashes of different colours, often in stripes, according to their states. Boots, rather than gaiters, were preferred by officers.

Because England's King was also Hanover's, German and British regiments had many weapons and accoutrements in common. The German musket, a copy of the Prussian one, was also of 0·75 calibre, pin-fastened, with brass furniture. Slings were of red-dyed leather, buckled at both ends. Unlike British troops, all ranks of German regiments carried short, brass-hilted hangers, mostly like the so-called pattern 1742 of the British. These were carried in black scabbards worn on a white waistbelt which was fastened with a frame brass buckle. Buckles were often false, the clasp inside the frame being what actually fastened the belt. Waterbottles were the same as those of the British.

From his left shoulder the German carried his cartridge-box on an extremely wide whitened leather sling. The box was equally large, usually bearing his prince's cypher on a large oval pewter plate fastened to the flap's centre. A small pocket on one end held the musket-pick.

From his other shoulder he slung his knapsack, a hairy cowhide affair closed with three buckles and leather straps. It was carried on a plain brown strap with a brass buckle to adjust its length and worn on the centre of the chest.

Battalion men wore cocked hats bound with white wool tape like the British, but usually with different coloured pompons worn over the black cockade and at the edge of the left cock. Small pewter- or brass-fronted caps, like those of British light infantry, bearing the prince's cypher, were worn by battalion men in fusilier regiments. Grenadiers wore much larger metal-fronted caps, with a worsted tassel on top and a bag of the regimental facing colour showing from the back. On fatigue duty, it would appear, they wore wool caps quite similar to those worn by the French in the last war.

Although German-made uniforms were quite good, the troops, when in the British service, were to be supplied by the British government, and quality was much poorer. Lapels were often simply pieces of coloured wool sewn down, in contrast to the German types which could be buttoned across the chest for warmth. One shipment of shoes sold to a German regiment turned out to be nothing but ladies' slippers.

Still, the Germans, plucked from their homes and sent to a strange land to fight a war they cared little about, fought as well as the professionals they were. Such a large war, and a civil war, such as this one in America, would need more than the small number of professionals – British and German – available. As with the last war, provincial troops would be needed.

*An engraved brass cartridge-box plate worn by regiments which had no unique badge of their own.* (Author's collection)

At first these were used for little more than police duties. In Boston garrison orders for 29 October 1775 it was noted that

'Some North British merchants residing here with their adherents having offered their services for the defense of the place, the Commander-in-Chief has order'd them to be armed and directed them to be formed into a company called "The Royal North British Volunteers". They will be distinguished by a blue bonnet with St. Andrews Cross upon it. Mr. James Anderson to be Captain, Wlm Blair and John Flemming, Lieutenants. The Guard Room and Alarm Post to be near Fennel Hall. The Company will mount a guard at Gunfiring and patrol the streets within a certain district and will take into custody any suspicious or disorderly persons found in the streets at improper hours.'

The unit was shortly followed by the Loyal American Association, who wore white sashes on their left arms; the Loyal Irish Volunteers, who wore white cockades in their hats; and Wentworth's Volunteers, who managed to obtain red coats.

These were certainly not complete uniforms, and this created problems. A Hessian officer reported that the King's Rangers, when posted on the outskirts of New York, '. . . as well as the New York and Grant's volunteer companies have repeatedly risked being fired upon, but since they resemble in many ways the rebels who have no uniform, the latter could not distinguish between friend and enemy'. Since the provincial regiments of this war, unlike those of the previous one, were being raised and supported not by the various colonial governments, but by the government in London, it fell upon London to supply their 'essentials and necessaries'.

Proper uniforms were both essential and necessary and, in 1776, the Army in New York received, to be issued to the provincials, 5,000 green coats faced white, green, and blue. These coats were lined with thin white wool, and four sergeants' and two drummers' coats were included with every 100 privates' coats. Pewter buttons with a crown and the letters RP, for Royal Provincial, were included, as were white waistcoats and breeches. Dark brown wool for leggings and 6,000 white stocks were sent as well. As more provincial units were raised, orange, black, and buff facings were added.

At the same time as the made-up regimental coats

were sent, some 6,000 yards of red wool, 'same as used for the marching regiments', was shipped over. This, too, was made into coats, so some regiments, like the Prince of Wales' American Regiment, started the war in red, not green, coats.

From a handful of loyal subjects offering their aid to the local commander, the provincial corps had grown to a regular set of regiments with strict structures. Typical of the beating orders raising them is the one issued to Lieutenant-Colonel George Wrightman, 21 March 1777:

'You are hereby authorized and empowered to raise for His Majesty's service, a Regiment of able-bodied men, to be composed of 30 Serjeants, 30 Corporals, Ten Drummers, and 500 Privates, divided into 10 Companies: each Company consisting of 1 Captain,

*Reconstructions of a period sergeant's and officer's uniforms. The sergeant wears his bayonet and sword-belt over his right shoulder.*

Each German regiment had one painted, silk colour, carried by an ensign. This one of the Brunswick Regiment von Rhetz is typical of most German designs. The ensign's cane is part of his rank identification. (Embleton/Osprey)

Breeches and leggings were replaced in the field by gaitered trousers, such as this grenadier of the Hesse-Hanau Regiment Erbprinz wears. Some were made from old tents, others of wool, and still others of bed-ticking. The grenadier's aiguilette appears to be a regimental distinction of the Erbprinz Regiment (Embleton/Osprey)

1 Lieut, 1 Ensign, 3 Serjeants, 3 Corporals, one drummer and 50 Privates, who will engage to carry arms under my orders, or the orders of the Commander in Chief of His Majesty's forces, for the time being, for two years, or if required during the continuance of the present Rebellion in North America: to receive the same pay, and be under the same discipline as His Majesty's Regular troops.

*This sergeant of the Royal Fencible Americans has a symbol of rank other than his plain lace, sash and hanger – a cane hanging from his button. The regiment was raised and stationed in Nova Scotia in 1775, serving there throughout the war. It was later issued with red-faced blue coats.* (Youens/ Osprey)

'The Officers are to be approved of by me, and their appointments by Commission, will depend on the success in Recruiting, they are to be instructed to raise the following numbers to entitle them thereto (vizt) a Captain, 30 men: a Lieut, 15 men; an Ensign, 12 men; and it is to be made known to them, that their pay will not commence until half the above number is raised and brought to the Rendezvous of the Recruits at Rhode Island.

'In like manner when one half the Corps is raised, mustered, and approved by a reviewing officer, a Major will be commissioned: and your Commission as a Lieut Colonel will be made out on 400 men being raised. In the meantime you will receive pay as a Captain until 250 men are raised: as a Major until 400 are raised: and as a Lieut Colonel from that period.

'Forty Shillings currency will be allowed as bounty for each man enlisted and approved.

'All officers civil and military, and others His Majesty's liege Subjects, are hereby required to be aiding and assisting unto you and all concerned in the Execution of the above service. For which this shall be to you and them a sufficient Warrent and Authority.'

Wrightman, orders in hand, headed for Newport, Rhode Island, where he set up his headquarters, expecting, no doubt, the recruits to flow in. They did not. On 28 July 1779, Provincial Muster Master Edward Winslow reported to Army headquarters:

'It is incumbent on me to observe that there is a corps called the Loyal New Englanders, commanded by Lieut Colonel Weightman, in which there are only fifty eight effectives, rank and file, altho. the warrant for raising this Corps has been granted above two years and the officers have been appointed for three Companies – For some time past its number of men has been diminishing, and since I have resided at Newport, not a single recruit has been added to this Corps.

'From the most particular observations I am satisfied there is not the least probability of the number being increased or of his Majesty's service being benefited by the continuance of this Corps.

'I therefore humbly submit to you, whether it may or may not be expedient to recommend that the few men who remain may be drafted into some other

*A Long Land Model Brown Bess, with the early wooden ramrod, as issued to some Provincial regiments. The lock is marked 'TOWER 1740'.* (George C. Neumann Collection)

Corps, and the officers seconded, as is usual in such cases.'

It was indeed usual and there were a number of such cases. The Queen's Loyal Virginians had taken quite a beating in Virginia, their home ground, and found themselves sent to New York where they were combined with the King's Rangers to form a new Queen's Rangers. On the whole, however, recruiting went well, with the colony of New York alone providing 23,500 men into the provincial corps. Men took their lives in their hands to flee rebel-held territories and enlist in the corps:

'Several times rebels have come into the English camp at night in small boats [wrote the Hessian adjutant-general in New York]. They were assigned to Colonel Delancy's new brigade, which is now two thousand strong. The colonel's ancestors settled on New York Island and he has suffered much from the rebels. Several Hundred of the prisoners taken in the action of the 27th of August have also been mustered into this brigade.'

Delancy's brigade eventually mustered three full battalions, although in a burst of enthusiasm at first, they recruited just about anybody who expressed an interest in joining. In early 1777 Colonel Delancy had to order that all Negroes and other 'improper persons' were to be discharged from the brigade at once.

Besides the regular provincial regiments formed to serve anywhere ordered, militia companies were formed to perform garrison duties in British-held territories. Of these territories New York was the largest, most populated, and longest held. It was there, naturally, that the largest militia was formed. The *New York Gazette and Mercury* reported on 20 November 1777:

'The indulgences of the Commander-in-Chief has prompted the principal gentlemen, inhabitants of

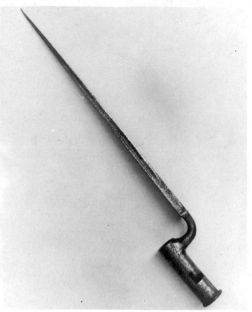

*Iron socket bayonet for the Brown Bess musket.* (Author's collection)

this city and refugees from other provinces, to form themselves into independent companies, twenty of which are nearly compleated. Last Monday several companies of them paraded on the fields, at the upper end of Broadway, headed by the Worshipful David Matthews, Esq., and made a very fine appearance. These companies, together with the militia, will greatly add to the strength of the city, and relieve the King's troops, who may be employed elsewhere.'

By July, 1781, the New York militia boasted some 3,500 men, including a company of artillery and artisans. Fifty dragoons were also organized for scouting and messenger duty.

Militia units were founded not just in the city, but in its suburbs as well. On Long Island, the Loyal Queen's County Militia was unusual in having a whole uniform described for its officers:

'Colonel Hamilton desires that the officers of the Regiment of Loyal Queen's County will provide themselves immediately each with a uniform or regimentals. It is to be scarlet, faced with blue, with white lining, white waistcoat and breeches, and silver buttons, with a silver epaulet, a well-cocked hat with silver buttons and loops and a silver hat band. Whatever officer appears upon and (does) duty without his regimentals or sidearms may depend upon being fined half a Joe for the entertainment of his fellow officers. . . .'

Regardless of the officers' splendour, the other ranks typically appeared for duty in whatever clothes they had on hand. A North Carolina militiaman in 1775 wore '. . . old buckskin breeches . . . and a long hunting shirt . . .'. Besides being poorly dressed, most militia units were badly armed. The Loyal Queen's County Militia received old muskets 'with wooden ramrods' and 'old cartridge-boxes' of Delancy's brigade.

*Left, the Battalion Colour and, right, the King's Colour, of the Queen's Rangers were similar in design to all those carried by British regiments of the period.* (James Ross Robertson Collection, Metropolitan Toronto Central Library)

Probably the only real battle that the militia engaged in on their own was when the Westchester Militia and Delancy's Refugees raided a grain and flour magazine near White Plains, New York, bringing off the entire store and some prisoners.

As might be expected, the militia was not well liked. The Provincial Inspector-General, Lieutenant-Colonel Alexander Innes, wrote: 'I look upon it that every man intitled to serve in a provincial corps during the war is a useful soldier gain'd to the King's Service and I am well convinced the Militia on their present plan will ever prove a useless, disorderly, distructive banditti.'

Although regulars might dislike the provincial militia, the regular provincial corps was getting better trained. As a mark of recognition of their growing abilities, in the winter of 1777, it was decided to put all the provincials into red coats, like the regulars. This may have been encouraging to some, but it had its other psychological side as well. The *New York Gazette* on 17 June 1778 reported that: 'The New Levies have changed their green coats for

The orange in the title of the King's Orange Rangers comes from the fact that the men came from Orange County, New York. The regiment was a mounted rifle regiment. Red coats with orange facings were later-issued. Orange was one of the most difficult colours there was to dye in that period, and the facings were actually any colour from yellow to a dirty reddish brown. (Youens/Osprey)

The Jamaica Volunteers was one of a number of units raised from free negroes and slaves freed from the American Colonies. They were equipped with the standard British kit, and fought the Spanish and French in the West Indies. The goatskin square-on-the-back knapsack can be seen here. (Youens/Osprey)

The King's American Regiment was probably one of the better
equipped provincial units raised. Officers commonly wore boots,
although if the men were wearing half gaiters they were supposed
to, too. The sword-belt, worn outside the coat, was the most
popular way of carrying the sword. (Youens/Osprey)

Each battalion of the New Jersey Volunteers spaced its buttons
differently according to its number. Gaitered trousers were
issued in winter in New York, made of blue, red, brown, and
green wool. (Youens/Osprey)

red ones, and Mr. Skinner's poor deluded followers begin now to see that this is but a prelude to their being drafted to fill up the British regiments.'

One provincial officer who fought to keep his men in green uniform was Lieutenant Colonel John Simcoe, commanding the Queen's Rangers. He succeeded, getting them green waistcoats as well. The men would wear the sleeved waistcoats during the summer, and their green regimental coats during the winter. 'Green', he wrote, 'is without comparison the best colour for light troops with dark accoutrements, and if it is put on in the spring, by autumn it nearly fades with the leaves, preserving its characteristics of being scarcely discernable at a distance.'

Simcoe's unit had quite a variety of troops wearing green. His 11th company,

*A contemporary sketch of a rifleman of the Queen's Rangers.* (John Ross Robertson Collection, Metropolitan Toronto Central Library)

'was formed of Highlanders . . . and the command was given to Captain M'Kay; they were furnished with the Highland dress, and their national piper, and were posted on the left flank of the regiment, which consisted of eight [battalion] companies, a grenadier and a light infantry company. [Later] Sergeant M'Pherson, a corporal and twelve men were selected and placed under the command of Lieutenant Shaw; they were armed with swords and rifles; and, being daily exercised in the firing at objects, soon became the most admirable and useful marksmen.'

Still later Simcoe converted one company into a troop of hussars.

*An engraved plate for the sword-belt of an officer of the 4th Battalion, New Jersey Volunteers.* (The New Brunswick Museum)

76

*A grenadier of the Queen's Rangers with the 'winged lappets' on his regimental coat which were popular with British militia units, and even some regular ones like the 101st Regiment of Foot.* (John Ross Robertson Collection, Metropolitan Toronto Central Library)

*A hussar and a light infantryman of the Queen's Rangers.* (John Ross Robertson Collection, Metropolitan Toronto Central Library)

A more important mark of recognition of how well the provincial corps were being trained and how valuable they had become was given in 1779 when the government created an 'American Establishment' and renamed Simcoe's unit the 1st American Regiment. The Volunteers of Ireland became the 2nd American Regiment, and the New York Volunteers, the 3rd. Later, on 7 March 1781, the King's American Regiment became the 4th American Regiment, and the British Legion, the 5th.

From this it was an easy step to being placed on the *Army Lists* as part of the regular British establishment. The Royal Highland Emigrants became the 84th Regiment of Foot, while the Volunteers of Ireland were now called the 105th Regiment of Foot. The British Legion, the Queen's Rangers, and the King's American Regiment were placed on the regular establishment under their old names. Another regiment, the Royal Garrison Regiment, was also placed on the regular establishment. This

regiment had been formed in New York in September 1778 from men of other regiments unable, due to wounds or illness, to serve on active duty.

Besides putting some few provincial regiments on the various establishments, the authorities formally spelled out the status of all provincial officers. They were to rank as junior to British officers of the same grade, but, if disabled in service, would receive the same pensions as British officers of their grade. What was more important, in terms of getting men to serve as officers, was the fact that when the war finally ended, and the provincial regiments disbanded, the officers would draw pensions of half the pay they were presently receiving, exactly as officers of disbanded British regiments.

They would be getting no more than they deserved. Campaigning through the American wilderness was no easier than it had been in the last war. Simcoe reported that when the new 1st American Regiment went down to Virginia in 1779, 'The

The Guides and Pioneers were uniformed as were the British Guides and Pioneers, although raised as part of the provincial corps. They were present at most of the major battles of the war, engaged in building fortifications, and clearing away enemy works. Their dress was highly functional for this type of work. (Youens/Osprey)

The Royal Highland Emigrants was raised in Canada from men who had been soldiers in stood-down Highland regiments of the previous war. It was later placed on the regular establishment as the 84th Regiment of Foot. In dress the men wore special sporrans patterned after those of the 42nd Regiment. As old Scottish soldiers, many probably carried broadswords, while the other Highland regiments relied on their muskets and bayonets. (Youens/Osprey)

Officers of the crack British Legion wore skin-tight breeches, boots, and jackets. The unit wore plain white dress in the summer campaigns in the south. It was one of the most active and feared units in the provincial corps. (Youens/Osprey)

Kilts and fly plaids from the 71st Regiment of Foot were issued to the North Carolina Highlanders. Their blue jackets were locally made. The rest of the kit is a typical Highland one. (Youens/Osprey)

*The engraved brass sword-belt plate of an officer of Butler's Rangers.* (Rebecca Katcher)

*Butler's Rangers took the usual plain cartridge-box plate and engraved its designation around the outside rim. A piece of red wool was generally worn under the brass plate.* (Rebecca Katcher)

incessant marches of the Rangers, and their distance from their stores, had so worn out their shoes that, on Lt. Colonel Simcoe's calling for a return, it appeared that near fifty men were absolutely bare-footed. . . .' Probably some of the barefooted men wore the regiment's new 'light caps, neat and commodious, in room of the miserable contract hats, which had been sent from England'.

Sent from England at the same time as the 'miserable contract hats' were drummers' coats of different colours, as per regimental facings, made like those of the regular regiments. Musicians' coats were made of the facing colour with red lapels, collars, and cuffs. These provincial coats were white, buff, orange, and black. The Queen's Rangers also received 'Knapsacks with buff belts. Canteens with strings for infantry, with belts for cavalry. Axes with cases and belts'.

The canteens with strings were probably the standard tin waterbottles, while those with belts were probably wooden ones, made like those the French had used in the last war. This type of canteen had been issued to cavalrymen in the British service as early as 1778.

A good number of the provincial units raised were mounted. Some of them, like the King's Orange Rangers, which was actually a rifle outfit, would ride to the scene of battle, dismount, and then fight on foot. Others were regular light cavalry or dragoon types of units. Three such companies were raised in Philadelphia: the Philadelphia Light Dragoons, the Bucks County Dragoons, and James's Troop of Dragoons. They were generally attached to other regiments, such as the Queen's Rangers, on active service and were therefore ordered into green coats to match those of the units they served with. The captain of at least one of the companies, however, always wore a red coat.

Towards the end of the war a number of the odd mounted units, and survivors of units captured in various campaigns, were combined into a new *élite* unit, the King's American Dragoons. An advertisement in the New York *Royal Gazette* in April 1782 called for '. . . likely and spirited young men desirous of serving their King and country and who prefer riding to going on foot'. Volunteers were offered a ten guinea bonus for enlisting.

The war, by this time, was practically over. The provincial corps was growing smaller by losses

and desertions, while the area controlled by British troops was shrinking – meaning that there were less people to recruit in their areas. On 21 May 1782 the new Commander-in-Chief in America, General Sir Guy Carleton, reviewed the King's American Dragoons, the American Legion, the Queen's Legion, the British Legion, and the Loyal American Regiment. He indicated that he was

'. . . extremely well satisfied; [but] since the provincial corps were so weak, however, the commanders were asked to look around diligently for recruits and send in without delay detailed accounts of the recruiting money received, how it was spent, and who received rations. This [said the Hessian adjutant-general] will cause much explanation. Later exact and detailed specifications were drawn up as to who is entitled to receive rations and who not. In order to prevent dishonesty, the receipts are countersigned in the districts where the troops are stationed.'

In October 1782 word reached America that Great Britain would recognize American Independence. The provincial corps was not instantly demobilized, and it was not until August 1783 that the Hessian Adjutant-General could report:

'Those who wish to remain in America have been ordered to draw pay until the 25th of October, and two weeks' maintenance and have been told to cross the lines in groups of three. Only a few have chosen to remain in America. Most of them desire to go to Nova Scotia, where the provincial corps noted below will be transported as units and where

*The stock issue button to provincial units which had no unique button is the top left one. The rest of these buttons are for: top, from left – the Queen's Rangers, 2nd American, New York Volunteers, and King's American Regiment; bottom row, from left – the King's Royal Regiment of New York, Butler's Rangers, the King's Orange Rangers, the 84th Regiment of Foot, and the King's American Dragoons. (Rebecca Katcher)*

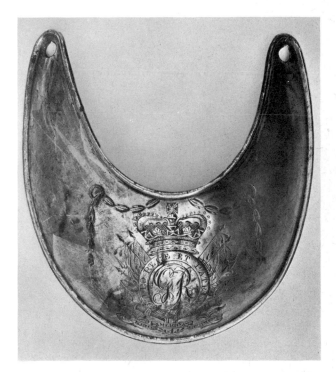

*A King's American Regiment officer's gorget. It was worn around the neck, hung by facing colour ribbon.* (Metropolitan Museum of Art)

Men of the Royal Garrison Battalion were unable to serve in active units for physical reasons. They were stationed both in New York and Bermuda. The men drew coats faced both blue and green, probably because their resupply was not high on the Quartermaster's priority list. Otherwise, their kit was typical issue. (Youens/Osprey)

The Newfoundland Regiment was raised in Newfoundland and placed on the regular establishment. Its entire service was spent in garrisoning the colony. The blue-faced red coats were originally intended for the Royal Artillery. Lace was plain white. The regiment was stood down after the war. (Youens/Osprey)

they will disband. None of them have been offered passage to England. The units are: Garrison Battalion, whose 1st Battalion is in the Bermudas; New York Volunteers; New Jersey Volunteers, all three battalions; Delancy's Brigade, 2nd and 1st Battalions; the Prince of Wales' American Regiment; Pennsylvania Loyalists; Maryland Loyalists; Guides and Pioneers.'

*The brass, engraved sword-belt plate of an officer of the King's American Dragoons.* (Rebecca Katcher)

Actually, the Garrison Regiment, because the men's poor health would have suffered greatly in the hard Canadian winters, was finally disbanded in England. The others, settled along the Canadian-United States border, would be ready to take up their arms again if the Americans were to want another war.

*Benjamin Thompson, commanding the King's American Dragoons, took an especial pride in the unit's dress. He made sure they were as well uniformed as any regular British regiment of dragoons. The unit was clad quite similarly to the 16th (Burgoyne's) Regiment of Light Dragoons, which had left America before Thompson's unit was formed.* (Youens/Osprey)

# 5

# The American Army 1775–1783

For many Americans of 1775 things were getting to the point of no return. The government in London seemed to be getting further and further out of touch with the feelings of the Americans they had so recently freed from the French threat. Now an American assembly, made up of everyone from radicals to men who were fairly conservative, filled the lofty, cool room off the main hall of the State House in Philadelphia. Outside, the street cries and the traffic noise in the second largest English-speaking city in the world, filtered through the big windows looking over dusty Chestnut Street.

Inside Captain George Washington, silent, tall, not quite comfortable in his ill-fitting false teeth, but every inch a soldier in the blue, buff-faced regimental coat of the Fairfax County Independent Company, had just been chosen to be 'Commander-in-Chief of the armies of the United Colonies, and all the forces now raised, or to be raised by them'.

It was 14 June 1775 and the United Colonies had, indeed, raised some armies, or if not armies, an assemblage of armed men which even now was hemming in a British army in the rebellious town of Boston.

Actually, only the most patriotic would call it an army. Every colony recruited and organized their own forces as it thought best. There might be a regiment of close to 1,000 men posted next to another with less than 200. It would take all of Washington's abilities first to create a real army and then, and only then, to face and beat the British Army. Thoughts on how to do this must have been foremost in his mind as he rode the rutted, dusty roads from Philadelphia north to Boston.

American military experience had been with the British, either as regulars or with the provincials of the last war. It was natural, therefore, that British military systems would be the ones copied. They still differed considerably from colony to colony.

Virginia's Convention of Delegates, for example, on 1 December 1775, augmented the colony's two militia regiments by adding 382 men, 'to be divided into five companies, consisting of sixty-eight men each rank and file, under the command of one captain, two lieutenants, one ensign, and four serjeants; each company to be allowed a drummer and fifer, and two of the said companies to be added to the first and the remaining three companies to the second regiment'. Furthermore, six new regiments were to be raised,

'. . . to be composed of ten companies of sixty-eight men each rank and file (three of which companies in each regiment to consist of riflemen, to act as light infantry) under the command of a colonel, lieutenant-colonel, a major, ten captains, twenty lieutenants, ten ensigns, forty serjeants, and to be allowed ten drummers and ten fifers; and to each of the said regiments there shall be moreover allowed a chaplain, an adjutant, a regimental quartermaster, one surgeon, two surgeons mates, one serjeant-major, one drum-major, and quarter-master's serjeant'.

The delegates then authorized a 'battalion of minute-men' to defend part of its territory, consisting of seven companies of sixty-eight men each, '. . . under command of a colonel, lieutenant-colonel, a major, seven captains, fourteen lieutenants, seven ensigns, twenty-eight serjeants, and each company to be allowed a drummer and fifer'. This battalion was to have two rifle companies, besides a chaplain and a paymaster.

Virginia's whole army was then to be placed under the command of a major-general, with two brigadier-generals, 'each of whom shall have an aide-de-camp and secretary of their appointment; and there be one quartermaster-general, one adjutant-general, and one deputy adjutant-general'.

Massachusetts wanted regiments of ten companies each of fifty rank and file, with a captain, lieutenant, ensign, four sergeants, a drummer and fifer, as did New Hampshire. Connecticut, on the other hand, started the war authorizing six battalions made up of ten companies each with 100 men, including a captain, two lieutenants and an ensign, and two battalions with companies of seventy men each. Rhode Island's regiments were to have eight, and later ten, companies of sixty men.

New York raised four regiments of 750 men, and the 'Green Mountain Boys', with 500 men. Each New York regiment was to have three field officers, an adjutant, a quartermaster, and a surgeon, and ten companies, each consisting of a captain, two lieutenants, three sergeants, three corporals, a drummer and a fifer, and sixty-four privates. The Green Mountain Boys had only two field officers and seven companies.

Pennsylvania originally raised a battalion of one rifle and seven battalion companies. On 15 December 1775 the colony's government decided to raise four more battalions of the same make-up. The Delaware Committee of Safety was to raise a single eight-company battalion, each company made up of a captain, three lieutenants, four sergeants, four corporals, a drummer and a bugler, and sixty-eight privates. The Maryland legislature created Smallwood's Regiment with eight battalion and one rifle, or light, company, in January, 1776. Each company had a captain, two lieutenants, an ensign, and sixty-eight privates.

North Carolina authorized two regiments, each with three field officers and 500 men. The Provincial Congress of South Carolina planned two infantry regiments and one of rangers. Each of the first two

*George Washington when serving as President. His odd expression is caused by ill-fitting false teeth.* (National Portrait Gallery)

regiments would be made up of a colonel, a lieutenant-colonel, a major, an adjutant, a quartermaster, a surgeon, two surgeon's mates, a sergeant-major, an armourer, an assistant armourer, five extra privates, and ten companies, including a grenadier company. Each company was to be made up of a captain, two lieutenants, three sergeants and three corporals, two drummers, and sixty-nine privates.

The ranger regiment was to have a lieutenant-colonel, a major, a surgeon, a paymaster, and nine companies each of a captain, two lieutenants, two sergeants, a drummer, and fifty corporals and privates. It was to be equipped with rifles and mounted, although actually many of the men seemed never to receive their rifles.

At the same time Georgia was raising a regiment of infantry consisting of a colonel, a lieutenant-colonel, a major, and eight companies, including a rifle company. Each company was to have a captain,

Minutemen were the first Continental forces. They were militia-men, agreed to turn out, 'on a minute's notice'. They had no particular uniform, but wore their civilian clothes. Each man was required to provide his own musket and bayonet or short sword. His hat was a safe place to carry his fragile clay pipe. (Roffe/Osprey)

Lapels of regimental coats were made to button over in cold weather, as is being done by this private of the Green Mountain Boys. The regiment was raised in what is now Vermont, then part of New York. Besides the green-faced red coats, the men wore buckskin breeches. The musket is a French one, possibly a relic of the previous war. (Roffe/Osprey)

*The sparsely settled southern states were hardest hit in uniforming and equipping their quotas of Continental troops. This private of the 1st Georgia has received a white linen hunting-shirt, but everything else has been brought from home and he has few hopes of ever seeing the blue coats with blue facings and white lace ordered by Washington for his state's uniform dress.* (Youens/Osprey)

two lieutenants, one ensign, four sergeants, four corporals, a drummer, and, hopefully for this small colony, at least forty-eight privates. That figure, however, was not reached and by April, 1776, only ten riflemen were recruited.

Other arms besides infantry would be needed, and Massachusetts had already raised an artillery regiment, made up of three staff officers and six companies. In November 1775 Henry Knox was named to command the regiment, which consisted of a lieutenant-colonel, a major, eight captains, nine captain-lieutenants, eight first lieutenants, seventeen second lieutenants, an adjutant, a quartermaster, a surgeon and his mate, a commissary, two clerks, four conductors, twenty-six sergeants, twenty-six corporals, fifty-two bombardiers, forty-nine gunners, eighteen fifers and drummers, and 257 matrosses.

*The 4th Pennsylvania Battalion of 1776 was one of the state's best-dressed units. Its first colonel was Anthony Wayne, a stickler for fine uniforms. This field officer of the battalion has provided himself with boots, which were quite popular among mounted officers. The battalion was designated the 5th Pennsylvania Regiment in 1777.* (Roffe/Osprey)

*A Continental musketman, as seen by a British cartoonist.*
(Metropolitan Museum of Art)

cut company, had full uniforms, in this case blue, red-faced regimental coats, but most of the men looked as if some huge eighteenth-century union of labourers, merchants, and students had called a strike meeting.

For instance, was the man talking to Washington a corporal, a brigadier-general, or a major of brigade? Washington quickly set out orders giving himself a pale blue ribbon, worn from his right shoulder to left hip, while other generals would wear pink ribbons. Aides-de-camp and majors of brigade would wear green ribbons. Later, major-generals received purple ribbons.

One thing common to just about all was the cocked hat, and officers were to be marked by cockades in their hats. Field officers were to obtain red or pink cockades, while captains had yellow ones, and subalterns had green. At least one lieutenant was arrested for '. . . assuming the rank of Captain, wearing a yellow cockade, and mounting Guard in that capacity'. In 1776 captains' cockades were changed to white or buff instead of yellow. Throughout the war, Continental officers do not appear to have worn sashes of any colour, although a few colonels wore red ones outside their coats from their right shoulders to their left hips.

Non-commissioned officers were to wear an epaulette, red for sergeants and green for corporals, on their right shoulders. Because it wasn't possible

Hardly any sort of regular army, and quite a problem for Washington. His first move, after arriving in its ramshackle camp, was to announce that he was in command of all the troops raised by the Continental Congress – not the troops of any one colony only, but those of the 'United Provinces of North America'.

This may have convinced some of the men in the mob outside Boston that they were, indeed, a Continental army, but they must have been few in number. Not only were they organized in every which way, but they simply didn't look like soldiers. Most of them had marched off in whatever civilian clothes they had on and as yet uniforms were not seen in any number. A few of the men like Washington were in pre-war units and wore their old uniforms; some units, like Captain Chester's Connecti-

*Saddlebags are hung on the rear of this saddle. Across the front is a pair of bearskin-covered holsters. The carbine-bucket hangs below the holster.*

*Scottish iron-hilted broadswords were highly popular as Continental dragoon sabres.*

to obtain enough epaulettes, non-commissioned officers were allowed simply to sew a stripe of the correct colour on their coats or hunting-shirts.

Washington then set up a board which numbered the regiments according to seniority, ending up with thirty-eight numbered Continental regiments of foot. These regiments had been enlisted for a year only, and after that year many of the men were ready to return to civilian life. Unfortunately for Washington and Congress, the British weren't quite as ready to return to civilian life, and a new army had to be recruited, organized, and trained – while all the time besieging Boston.

In the new Continental Army each infantry regiment was to have a colonel, a lieutenant-colonel, a major, an adjutant, a quartermaster, a surgeon and his mate, a chaplain, and eight companies, each one with a captain, two lieutenants, an ensign, four sergeants, four corporals, a drummer and a fifer, and seventy-six privates. In July, 1776, this number was increased by adding a sergeant-major, a quartermaster-sergeant, and both a drum-major and a fife-major.

A problem in dealing with a Continental Army is that it isn't just one army; it is a number of different ones. There is the mob which gathered around Boston in 1775. There are the numbered Continental regiments of foot, mostly taken from

New England, in 1776. There are the various state lines which served from 1777 until about Yorktown in 1781. And, finally, there is the ever-smaller group of regiments which lasted until peace was declared in 1783. A number of men served in virtually all these organizations while others would drop out for a season and return later, or perhaps never return.

There was, however, that hard core of men who followed Washington. On 16 September 1776 Congress resolved that eighty-eight infantry battalions should be enlisted for the war's duration. New Hampshire was to supply three regiments, while Massachusetts was to supply fifteen. Little Rhode Island was to supply two regiments and Connecticut, eight. New York and New Jersey were to supply four regiments each. Pennsylvania would supply twelve regiments, while its small neighbour, Delaware, could supply only one. Further south, Maryland was to come up with men for eight regiments and Virginia for fifteen. North Carolina would have nine and South Carolina, six. Georgia, the smallest colony, would supply men and equipment for one regiment.

Numbered Continental Regiments of Foot simply

*Although French muskets were the most favoured, mounted men preferred British pistols, like this 0·65-calibre model. These were smoothbore, but some American-made pistols had rifled barrels.* (George C. Neumann Collection)

The Continental artillery regiments were to have the most elaborate uniform ordered for any Continental unit. A few early artillery units used different colour schemes, but dark blue faced red and laced with yellow was the most popular and officially ordered for the corps in 1779. Artillerymen carried full infantry accoutrements and muskets for personal defence. (Roffe/Osprey)

By 1779 the 3rd Continental Dragoons wore sky-blue facings on white coats. Their caps were decorated leather 'jockey caps'. This private carries a set of plain leather saddlebags, in which he carries all his spare clothing. (Roffe/Osprey)

The 1st Continental Dragoons in 1778 wore this type of uniform, although previously they had worn blue coats with red facings. In 1780 blue coats with green facings seem to have been standard. The fully equipped dragoon has a carbine, sword, and two pistols. (Roffe/Osprey)

took state designations, and completed their state's quota. For example, the 1st Pennsylvania Battalion of 1775 became the 1st Continental Regiment of Foot in 1776 and then the 2nd Pennsylvania Regiment in 1777. Under this designation it served through to the war's end. On the other hand, Colonel David Forman's Additional Continental Regiment, raised in 1777, was dissolved and the men simply assigned where needed in all four New Jersey regiments in July, 1778.

Forman's ill-fated regiment, by the way, seemed to have been largely supplied with the red, buff-faced coats and buff breeches and waistcoats captured from British supply ships bound for the 31st Regiment of Foot, then in Canada. That was one way of settling the uniform problem.

It was, in fact, far from an uncommon way of dealing with the serious problem of getting this large body of men into uniform. An artillery sergeant after the battle of Princeton found a room in the college building with breakfast waiting on the table. After helping himself, he, '. . . looked round the room, and saw an officer's coat – I went to it, and found it a new one; the paper never taken off the buttons, was plated or solid silver, I could not determine which, lined with white satin . . .'. Later, 'The coat I sold to an officer of an rifle regiment (the uniform answered to his description but for the buttons; it belonged to the 40th regiment, faced with white) for 18$. That regiment all the commissioned officers wore red coats, faced with white. . . .'

The Army was growing, getting organized. Now that regiments were pretty well standardized, larger units, easier to administer and manœuvre, would have to be set up. Brigades were organized, and brigadier-generals appointed to command them.

The exact size of a Continental brigade varied greatly. Woodford's Virginia Brigade – brigades were usually geographical in make-up – consisted of only the 7th and 11th Virginia Regiments. All nine North Carolina regiments, admittedly smaller than most northern regiments, made up McIntosh's North Carolina Brigade. Four regiments, however, made up the typical brigade, such as Wayne's with the 1st, 2nd, 7th, and 10th Pennsylvania Regiments; Glover's with the 1st, 4th, 13th, and 15th Massachusetts Regiments; and Maxwell's with the four New Jersey Regiments. The artillery brigade consisted of the four regiments of the Continental Artillery.

Artillery regiments had been standardized on 27 May 1778 and were to be made up of a colonel, a lieutenant-colonel, a major, a surgeon and his mate, a sergeant-major, a quartermaster-sergeant, a fife-major, a drum-major, and twelve companies. Each company consisted of a captain, a captain-lieutenant, a first lieutenant, three second lieutenants, six sergeants, six bombardiers, six corporals, six gunners, four drummers and fifers, and fifty-six matrosses.

Besides the four Continental artillery regiments, there were some independent artillery units, like Steven's Independent Battalion of Artillery from New York and Coren's Independent Company of Artillery from Pennsylvania. The four Continental regiments were artillery enough for the main Continental Army, as may be judged from Henry Knox's estimate of the Continental artillery for the 1778 campaign:

*Left, the two colours carried by the 2nd Continental Dragoons, and, right, the last colour carried by the 3rd Continental Dragoons. The latter was carried during the southern campaigns and is said to have been made from a damask curtain.*

*Iron ice-creepers were attached to soldiers' shoes for walking on slippery streets.* (Author's collection)

'Brigade artillery, seventeen brigades, with four guns each, sixty-eight pieces to be 3, 4, or 6-pounders; with the park, two 24-pounders, four 12-pounders, four 8-inch howitzers, eight $5\frac{1}{2}$ inch howitzers, ten 3 or 4-pounders, ten 6-pounders; for the *reserve*, to be kept at a proper distance from camp, thirty 3, 4, and 6-pounders, two 12-pounders, one 24-pounder; all the foregoing brigade, park and reserve guns and howitzers *to be of brass*. In addition, twelve 18-pounders, twelve 12-pounders, battering pieces, on travelling carriages, together with two $5\frac{1}{2}$-inch and twelve 8, 9, and 10-inch mortars; the battering pieces and mortars to be of *cast-iron*.'

By 'brigade artillery', as opposed to the 'park' and 'reserve', Knox referred to the typical arrangement in the Continental Army where four guns from the different artillery regiments accompanied each infantry brigade. The Continental Artillery rarely fought with massed guns on any actions with anything larger than a company in action together.

American artillerymen considered themselves to be the same sort of trained *élite* as European artillerymen and adopted their uniform colours, generally, a blue coat faced red and trimmed with yellow. In May 1775 Joseph White was enlisted in what became the 1st Continental Artillery Regiment. He was soon made assistant adjutant, and then '. . . bought a uniform coat of an officer, he had when he belonged to capt. Paddock's company of artillery in Boston, but not the uniform of our regiment; the button holes and hat were trimmed with gold lace'.

Perhaps in detail it was not '. . . the uniform of our regiment', but in overall appearance it must have been quite similar. Coats for virtually every artillery regiment until Continental uniforms were standardized in 1779 seem to have been dark blue with red collars, cuffs, and lapels, white waistcoats and breeches, black cocked hats, and buttons of pewter or brass. The exception to this rule – and in the Continental Army there are as many exceptions as rules – seem to be New York's artillerymen. Lamb's Artillery Company, which made up the basis of the 2nd Artillery Regiment, used white or light buff facings. Steven's Independent Battalion, independent in dress as well as name, seemed to prefer a variety of coats, although brown with red facings was probably the most common.

In October 1779 Washington published orders establishing a common uniform for the whole Continental Army. The artillery was to wear dark blue coats with scarlet cuffs, collars, lapels, and linings. The facings were to be trimmed in yellow worsted lace, as were the buttonholes, and buttons were to be brass. Most commonly, Continental artillery buttons featured a cannon and flag on the large ones and a mortar on the small ones – both made of pewter. These were probably worn on the 1779 regulation coats as well as earlier ones, and such brass ones as were worn were probably plain.

Besides four regiments of artillery, Congress allowed the raising of four regiments of light dragoons. The 2nd Regiment of Continental Light Dragoons had been formed in late 1776 around a troop of Connecticut light horse, and was actually the first mounted regiment authorized by Congress. In January 1777 Congress ordered Theodoric Bland to form the 1st Regiment of Continental Light Dragoons, George Baylor, the 3rd, and Stephen Moylan, the 4th.

Regiments were to consist of a colonel, a lieutenant-colonel, a major, an adjutant, a quartermaster, a paymaster, a surgeon and his mate, a chaplain, a saddler, a riding master, a trumpet-major, and four supernumeraries armed with swords and pistols. Then the regiment would have six troops each made up of a captain, a lieutenant, a cornet, a quartermaster-sergeant, an orderly or drill sergeant, four corporals, a trumpeter, a farrier, an armourer, and thirty-two privates.

In 1778 each troop was ordered to recruit fifty-four privates, raising the number of officers and men in each regiment from 280 to 416. In 1781 the regimental structure was changed to that of a

The Corps of Light Infantry was about the most active unit in
the Continental service, and its dress had to be serviceable and
comfortable. Linen gaitered trousers, called overalls, and a linen
hunting-shirt were preferred. The caps were often made from
cut-down tricornes, but were usually leather. The musket is a
Dutch one, purchased by the Continental Congress.
(Roffe/Osprey)

The 2nd Canadian Regiment, of which this corporal is a
member, is also known as 'Congress' Own', because it
represented no particular state. Most of its members came from
Canada and Pennsylvania. Hats in the battalion companies
were bound up with white braid. In 1779 the white facings
were changed to red. (Roffe/Osprey)

Although musicians of the Continental Army were to wear their regiment's facings reversed, this fifer of Captain Robert Johnston's company of the 3rd New York Regiment has only managed to obtain a regular private's coat of his company. He wears an old-pattern waistcoat and trousers, which were quite popular with American troops. His hanger is American made. (Roffe/Osprey)

The Pennsylvania State Regiment was first organized for the state's defence, but later released for Continental service. It had both musket- and riflemen, with the musketmen wearing blue coats with both red and white facings, depending on what was available when they were made. The blanket roll was a common substitute for a regular knapsack. (Roffe/Osprey)

95

'legionary corps', with four mounted and two dismounted troops, the latter having drummers instead of trumpeters. The regiments were each also raised to 455 officers and men.

The cavalry's major weapon was the sabre. William Washington, commander of the 3rd Regiment, called the sword the '. . . most destructive and almost the only necessary weapon a Dragoon carries'. The typical Continental cavalry sabre had a slightly curved blade some thirty-six inches long, with a flat-sided blade and an iron stirrup-guard hilt. A number of Scottish broadswords also saw Continental dragoon service. Besides his sword, the cavalryman was armed with a pair of large pistols in saddle-holsters, which were mostly copies of British ones, captured or bought from continental Europe. When fighting dismounted, or standing still on his horse, the cavalryman used his third weapon, the carbine. Carbines were the same as muskets, but shorter and lighter. British and French models were the most common and American gunsmiths do not seem to have made many, if any, carbines.

Although the rest of the Army had its dress standardized in 1779, the four dragoon regiments continued to wear different uniforms from each other. The 1st wore short brown wool coats with green lapels, cuffs, and collars, green waistcoats,

*A contemporary drawing of, left, a Continental infantryman and, right, a Continental general.* (Michael D. Robson)

breeches of leather, yellow buttons, black leather caps with perpendicular fronts, and green turbans with yellow tassels. Trumpeters, saddlers, and farriers wore the coat colours reversed. About 1780 the uniform seems to have been changed to dark blue coats faced green and lined blue, with blue overalls for both the mounted and dismounted troops. Their black leather helmets had black cockades on the left side, although many men lacked helmets and had to wear cocked hats.

The 2nd seems to have worn blue coats with buff collars, cuffs, and lapels, buff waistcoats and breeches, and metal helmets with dark blue turbans and yellow tassels. Brown and dark-coloured overalls were worn by dismounted troops.

The 3rd which seems to have had the nickname of 'Lady Washington's Dragoons', wore white coats with light blue collars, cuffs, and lapels, black leather belts, and silver trimmings for officers. About 1780, when the regiment was sent south, it drew green facing cloth and leather breeches. Its helmets were trimmed with red turbans and a foxtail was added for decoration.

The 4th received captured red coats faced dark blue, taken from men of the 8th and 24th British Regiments of Foot. The officers had previously gone to 'considerable expence' to obtain scarlet uniforms. In 1780 the uniform was changed to a green coat faced red with red waistcoats and leather breeches and green overalls. Helmets were trimmed with bearskin and in foul weather they wore green cloaks with red capes.

If foul weather caught the poor infantryman he simply suffered. Wrote a veteran of years of service in the 6th Connecticut Regiment, the Corps of Light Infantry and the Corps of Sappers and Miners:

'Almost every one has heard of the soldiers of the Revolution being tracked by the blood of their feet on the frozen ground. This is literally true, and the thousandth part of their sufferings has not, nor ever will be told. That the country was young and poor, at that time, I am willing to allow, but young people are generally modest, especially females. Now, I think the country (although of the feminine gender, for we say "she" and "her" of it) showed but little modesty at the time alluded to, for she appeared to think her soldiers had no private parts. For on our march from Valley Forge, through the Jerseys, and at the boasted Battle of Monmouth, a fourth part of the troops had not a strip of anything but their ragged shirt flaps to cover their nakedness, and were obliged to remain so long after. I had picked up a few articles of light clothing during the past winter, while among the Pennsylvania farmers, or I should have been in the same predicament. "Rub and go" was always the Revolutionary soldier's motto.'

This is not simply the jaundiced view of one embittered individual. A lieutenant of the Pennsylvania State Regiment, after the battle of Long Island, wrote home: 'I wish you would endeavour to send me such of my clothes as are worth wearing . . . there are no clothes to be got here of any kind. I have lost all my shirts and stockings except two shirts and two pairs of stockings.' Help was the cry

*Top, a pair of officer's silver knee-buckles, while the bottom two pairs are types worn by other ranks.* (Author's collection)

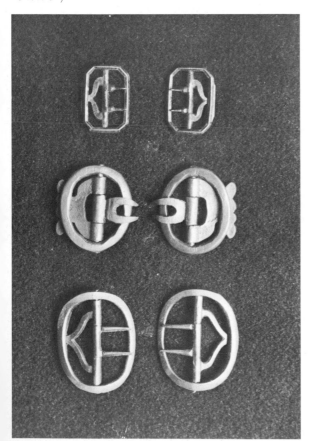

*A contemporary drawing of a Continental light infantry cap.*

from the Army, both from individuals to those at home and from commanding officers to their state legislatures. While the lieutenant wanted anything 'worth wearing', his commander, Colonel Samuel Atlee, was writing to the legislature that the 'battalion is without either shirts, Breeches or Stockings'. Even a year later the new commander, Colonel Walter Stewart, was still writing to the Pennsylvania legislature: 'My hopes of getting the Regiment genteelly and well cloathed this campaigne are vanished unless your Excellency and the Council will assist me in it.'

Not, of course, that every commanding officer was so conscientious in bombarding the folks back home with letters pleading for assistance. Washington himself was forced to write to the commanding officer of the 3rd Virginia Regiment in 1777:

'I am informed, and indeed I have observed, that the men of your Regiment are so exceedingly bare of necessaries, that it not only contributes to their unhealthiness but renders them absolutely unfit to take the Field. Inattention to the wants of Soldiers marks the bad Officer; it does more, it reasonably removes that confidence on which the Officers Honour and Reputation must depend.

'As there is Clothing now here, I desire you may immediately cause inquiry to be made into what is wanting, and make returns, that if the things are not here, they may be ordered on. If advantage is not taken to supply the Men, now we have a little leisure time, they will be miserable and naked during the active part of the Campaign.'

What were the necessaries to be given to the men? According to the Connecticut veteran:

For a short time several units of 'Flying Camp' served with the main Continental Army. Really little more than militia, the men, such as this member of the Pennsylvania Flying Camp, wore their own civilian clothing with weapons and accoutrements brought from home. The only attempt at uniformity which seems to have been made was the blue cockades the Delaware Flying Camp wore in their hats. (Youens/Osprey)

General Anthony Wayne, commanding the Corps of Light Infantry, was careful to make sure all his officers, such as this field officer, carried spontoons instead of fusils. Men of the corps wore their regular regimental uniforms and this man wears the facings of the middle Atlantic states. Later red and black plumes, to be worn over the caps' cockades, were awarded to all corps members. (Roffe/Osprey)

'They were . . . promised the following articles of clothing per year. One uniform coat, a woolen and a linen waistcoat, four shirts, four pairs of shoes, four pair of stockings, a pair of woolen and a pair of linen overalls, a hat or a leather cap, a stock for the neck, a hunting shirt, a pair of shoe buckles, and a blanket. Ample clothing, says the reader; and ample clothing, say I. But what did we ever realize of all this ample store – why, perhaps a coat (we generally did get that) and one or two shirts, the same of shoes and stockings, and, indeed, the same may be said of every other article of clothing – a few dribbled out in a regiment, two or three times in a year, never getting a whole suit at a time, and all of the poorest quality, and blankets of thin baize, thin enough to have straws shot through without discommoding the threads.'

The hunting-shirt mentioned was the first and easiest thing to get on everyone, to create some sort of uniform. On 24 July 1776 Washington wrote that 'No dress can be cheaper, nor more convenient, as the wearer may be cool in the warm weather and warm in cool weather by putting on under-cloaths

*The cartridge-box on top is made with tin tubes and used by mounted men, worn around the waist. The one at the bottom has a linen sling from which a pick and brush is hung. A wooden block in the box holds the ammunition.*

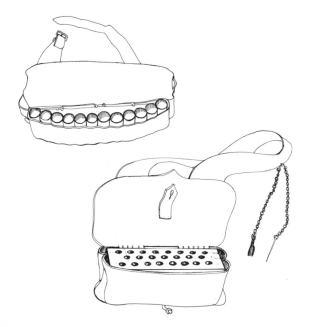

*Nicholas' battalion of Continental Marines was stationed with the main Continental Army from December 1776 until the fall of Fort Mifflin. The men's uniforms are believed to have been captured British ones intended to have been issued to provincials. The extra buttons on each cuff are the traditional ones on seafaring men's coats of that period. (Roffe/Osprey)*

which will not change the outward dress, Winter or Summer – Besides which it is a dress justly supposed to carry no small terror to the enemy, who think every such person (so dressed) is a complete marksman.'

The hunting-shirt itself was usually left its natural, tannish colour. Often it was dyed different colours for unit identification, however, such as dark blue in the 3rd New Jersey Regiment. At other times the shirt would be made with military badges or mottoes, like the 'Liberty or Death' on the fronts of those worn by the Culpepper Minute Battalion of Virginia. The 6th Virginia Regiment, in 1776, ordered that 'Captains . . . together with the other officers, . . . [are] immediately to provide themselves with Hunting Shirts, short and fringed; the men's shirts to be short and plain, the Sergeants' shirts to have small white cuffs and plain; the Drummers' shirts to be with dark Cuffs.'

Even with all the hunting-shirt's advantages, the men actually preferred the formal regimental coat, so identified with 'real soldiering' and taken in design from that of the British. Basically, the coat itself was made of heavy wool, with the same sort of collars, lapels and cuffs as the British design. At times only the skirts were lined, usually in a thinner white wool, but often the entire body was lined in thin wool or linen.

Lieutenant Abraham Chittenden described his 7th Connecticut's regimental coat in 1780:

'The uniform of the Regt. is to be blue with white facings, white vest and white Breeches: The officers are Desired to have their coats in exact uniform and are to observe the following directions in the fashion of them: Common round cuffs, 4 large buttons on each, common mode of pockets with four buttons on each, 4 buttons on each fold. Lappels $2\frac{1}{2}$ inch broad, with Lappets [small additions to the lapels which buttoned over the collar]; Button holes to the Lappets, and 10 Buttons to each equally divided plain behind and Laped over.'

Such a coat may seem an expensive piece of clothing, but orders for the 7th on 7 June 1782 called for the cost of, 'A full trimmed regitl Coat – 1 dollar & $\frac{1}{3}$'.

Besides the long regimental coat, short jackets were quite common. At one point, when supplies were quite low at Valley Forge, Washington ordered all the men to get tail-less jackets, which would button with a single row of buttons across the chest. Only the collars, made of different colours of wool, would show the different regiments.

These jackets were similar to those worn by seamen and were often called 'sailors' jackets'. Judging from the number mentioned in various deserter descriptions, it is quite possible that such jackets were at least as common, if not more so, than the full regimental coat – at least for the first two-thirds of the war.

It had been noted that the colonials did like brown coats, and so it was that Washington and Congress immediately agreed that the Continental troops should wear brown coats, with different facings. As most Connecticut and Massachusetts men were already wearing such coats, this was an easy decision.

Troops coming from further south, however, seemed to prefer blue as their basic colour. Probably the best equipped unit in the Army at its beginning, the Delaware Battalion, appeared thus at the start as described by a Hessian officer, 'in their blue and red coats'. Three of the first regiments from Pennsylvania wore brown coats, with white, green, and red facings, but regiments like the Pennsylvania State Regiment, the 4th Pennsylvania Battalion, and troops raised later immediately adopted blue coats. From New Jersey to Georgia, blue was the chosen colour. Rather than fight the trend, Con-

*Maryland issued tin waterbottles, made like the standard British ones, to its troops.* (Author's collection)

gress allowed the use of blue coats to those who had chosen them. From 1777 onwards blue was pretty much the standard regimental coat colour in the main Continental Army.

At the same time, however, one would also find regiments like the 3rd New York and some Maryland Regiments in grey coats; there were large numbers of men in captured red coats; green coats were worn by the Dover Light Infantry Company, the Green Mountain Boys, and others; in short, virtually any combination of colours you might want could be seen in the Continental Army.

In September 1778 some 20,000 regimental coats were received from France, all faced red with brown and blue bodies. The various state lines received either the brown or blue coats according to a lottery. Blue coats ended up in the hands of men from North Carolina, Maryland, New Jersey, and New York, while brown coats went to the regiments of Virginia, Delaware, Pennsylvania, Massachusetts, and New Hampshire, and to the 1st Canadian Regiment.

In October 1779, seeking to make some order out of this chaos, Washington set up a uniform dress regulation for the entire Army. All coats were to be blue, and facings would differ by groups of states. White facings went to New Hampshire, Massachusetts, Rhode Island, and Connecticut; buff to New York and New Jersey; Pennsylvania, Delaware, Maryland, and Virginia to have scarlet facings. The southern colonies were to have blue facings, with white bindings on all buttonholes. In each case, musicians were to wear the reverse of their regiment's colours.

It is one thing to write a set of orders – it is another thing to enforce them, especially in such a poorly supplied force as the Continental Army. Many officers got their newly ordered coats almost immediately, but it took longer to supply the men. Washington, of course, wanted to put on a quite proper, military appearance when the French Regulars arrived, and he finally had to write the commander of the Pennsylvania Line, among others, ordering him to get the necessary red material to replace his soldiers' old facings. In a letter to Pennsylvania's president, the General estimated it would take four days completely to convert all the old, multi-coloured facings in his line to the correct colour – if supplies were obtainable.

And supplies were certainly not always obtainable. In Philadelphia, headquarters of the Continental Clothier-General, blue cloth was not 'procurable at any Rate or Price'. The Pennsylvania Line had to cut their coat-tails off, making three good patched short coats from 'three old, tattered long ones'.

In 1783, what was left of the Continental Army was ordered into coats all blue faced red, although

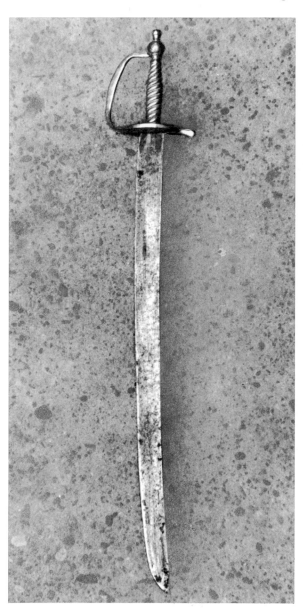

*British hangers, such as this brass-hilted 1742-pattern one, were widely used by Continental sergeants and musicians.* (Author's collection)

this may not have been wholly possible as many men continued to wear white facings.

In August, 1782, Washington ordered that each enlisted man who had served more than three years 'with bravery, fidelity and good conduct' could wear a 'narrow piece of white cloth, of an angular form' on the upper left arm of his coat. After six years the man was allowed to wear a parallel line. Later the stripes were to be made of the facing colours.

Besides his shirt and coat, each man was to receive 'a pair of woolen and a pair of linen overalls'. These were gaitered trousers, covering the shoe top and buttoning up the outside of the calf. They were to be tightly fitting, although as with most military clothing, tailoring was not of the best. In 1782 Washington reviewed his Connecticut troops and reported to their commanding officer that: 'The General could not avoid feeling some concern that all the Clothing did not appear perfectly fitted to the men, particularly overalls. He wishes these defects may be remedied as early and fully as possible.'

Overalls, at least later in the war when the Pennsylvanian Colonel Thomas Craig reported that his men 'were marched away in a linen Hunting Shirt, Overalls and Vest of the same', were usually linen. Virginia troops received brown linen, usually, white linen being reserved for shirts.

Neck stocks were usually black, although some Pennsylvanians early in the war may have been issued with red ones, and white ones are also reported. They were made of velvet, heavy horse hair, or leather. The leather ones were tied in back with heavy thongs usually, while others were buckled.

Hats, if possible, differed more widely than coats. The basic headgear was the cocked hat, which was sometimes bound with worsted tape, some regiments like the Pennsylvania State Regiment using yellow, although white was more common. All the hats remaining today, however, appear never to have been bound, so binding was probably rare. Cocked hats generally followed the British design.

Knitted wool caps were also quite popular. The 3rd Virginia Regiment received both 'double' and 'single' woollen caps in September 1778. Deserters from the 2nd and 4th New York Regiments were mentioned as wearing 'small round woolen hat(s).' One dug up from a Continental Army camp site is dull brown, some $6\frac{1}{4}$ in. high, 10 in. in diameter, with a 2 in. double brim.

Infantry regiments sometimes wore leather caps. The 1st and 2nd South Carolina Regiments wore leather caps with small visors. Colonel Walter Steward, of the 2nd Pennsylvania Regiment, wanted leather caps for his regiment 'in the same Pattern as colo. Megg's'. Colonel Meigs commanded the 6th Connecticut Regiment. Steward wanted the caps because 'my men at present . . . (are) very much in Want of them & Suffering Exceedingly on Account of the Warm Woolen Caps they are oblig'd Many of them to wear'.

Leather caps were worn by another body of men, the Corps of Light Infantry. In May 1778 Washington and Congress decided to reorganize each infantry regiment, to give it nine instead of eight companies, the new company being a light infantry company. It would be drawn from men of the other companies. During a campaign, the various light companies would be formed together to form the Corps of Light Infantry. In winter quarters they would stay with their own regiments. The corps was divided into four regiments of two battalions each, nearly 1,400 men. Some regiments already had light companies, and simply supplied them to the corps, while others drew men equally from each of their companies.

Generally, light infantrymen wore their old regimental uniform, although these may have been changed, for example by cutting the tails short. One woman, who not only managed to enlist but actually became a light infantryman, wrote that she received in 1781 the regulation New England blue-faced white uniform coat, a white waistcoat, and white breeches or overalls, but her coat was decorated also with white wings on the shoulders and white cords on the arms and pockets. She wore a cap with a cockade on one side, a red-tipped plume on the other, and a white turban around the whole thing.

The red-tipped plume probably dated from 1780 when the Marquis de Lafayette, who was then commanding the corps, presented each man in the corps with a black, hard leather, fur-crested helmet with a red and black plume. Besides the caps, he gave each man a French grenadier's hanger – all at his own expense.

Pennsylvania's light infantrymen, besides, were issued with another unique item. In August 1778 an entry in the 1st Pennsylvania Regiment's orderly book reads: 'The Tin Cannisters are to be put into

*Men of Daniel Morgan's rifle company came from the frontiers of Virginia. Self-reliant, they brought their own Pennsylvania rifles from home. Their fringed hunting-shirts and trousers were made of white linen. Powder was carried in a powder-horn, and balls in a leather bullet-bag.* (Roffe/Osprey)

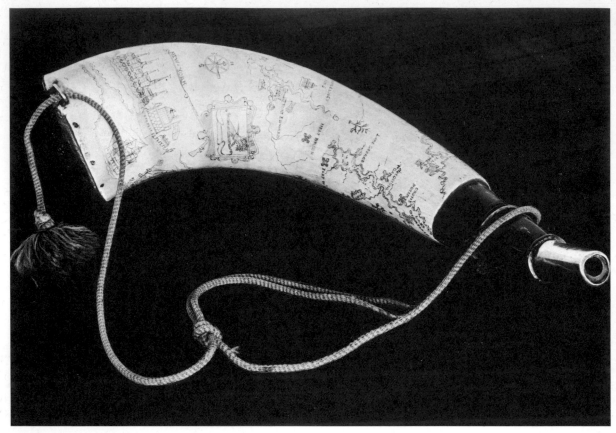

*The average rifleman carried his own powder-horn, in which he carried loose powder. Most of these were engraved by their owners with scenes of their campaigns or various symbols.*

the hands of those men who are in the light Infantry.' These tin canisters were a desperate attempt to get solid, waterproof carriers for ammunition to the men. They were 6½ in. deep, about 4 in. square, and held some thirty-six paper-wrapped cartridges. They appear to have been japanned black, possibly with some sort of unit device on their fronts. According to the Continental Board of War: 'The soldier carries a cannister by the shoulder belt, as he does a cartridge box.' All the states were recommended to supply them to their troops, although not all went to light infantrymen. Maryland, for example, seems to have issued them to sergeants as spare ammunition-carriers.

Anything like the tin canister which would carry ammunition safe and dry would be a great help. The typical Continental cartridge-box consisted of nothing more than a leather bag holding a block of

wood bored out for a number of cartridges and covered with a single leather flap. They were often suspended on linen slings because of the lack of leather, and even painted linen flaps seem to have been used. A Continental officer in 1780 wrote his commanding general that he had just received 300 'cartouch' boxes, and, he could, 'assure you they are not worthy of the name. Numbers of them are without any straps, others without flaps and scarce any of them would preserve the cartridges in a moderate shower of Rain – what straps there are to the boxes are of linen.'

Getting cartridges wet in the rain was a real problem. A British officer wrote that a pending battle, in late 1777, was called off because of heavy rain. 'The Violence of the Rain was so lasting that it was afterward known that the Rebels had not a single Cartridge in their Pouches but what was Wet.'

The soldier wore his cartridge-box on his right hip, and on the other was his bayonet-belt. It, too, was quite often of linen, although leather was preferred, and it was generally worn across the body instead of around the waist. Bayonet-scabbards and belts were so scarce that at least one time Washington had to order his soldiers to keep their bayonets constantly fixed.

On the march, Continentals carried canteens, too. Maryland troops were given tin canteens, like British ones, and at least one of these, used by a New York militiaman in 1777, still exists.

The wooden canteen appears to be the type most commonly used. It was generally between six and nine inches in diameter and some three inches thick. Usually it was bound with wooden hoops, although some iron-bound specimens might have seen service. Metal hoops were not common or popular until after the war. The canteens were usually unpainted.

Besides his canteen, the Continental carried a natural-coloured linen haversack. His rations and, perhaps, some spare ammunition were carried in this bag, which was closed with several plain buttons.

On his back he carried a knapsack, often of painted linen, and also closed with several buttons. In it would go his spare clothing, along with a blanket. Often he simply did away with the knapsack, wrapping shirts or whatever in the centre of his blanket which he rolled into a long, tight roll slung over his shoulder.

Not all knapsacks contained so little that they could be discarded for a blanket roll. The sergeant-major of Congress' Own Regiment at the battle of Brandywine lost his knapsack, 'which contained the following articles, viz: 1 uniform coat, brown faced with white; 1 shirt; 2 pair stockings; 1 sergeant's sash; 1 pair knee buckles; $\frac{1}{2}$ lb. soap; 1 orderly book; 1 memo book of journal and state of my company; 1 quire paper; 2 vials ink; 1 brass inkhorn; 40 morning returns, printed blanks; 1 tin gill cup; a letter and a book.'

Troops from Virginia, Maryland, Pennsylvania,

*The iron head of a typical six-foot spontoon.* (Author's collection)

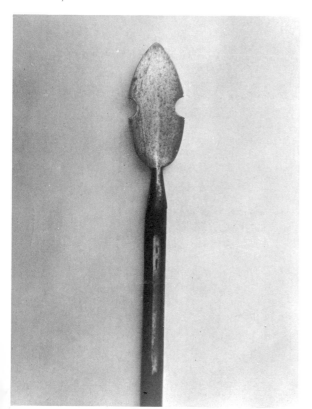

*Many Continental sergeants carried halberds, such as this British one, as symbols of their rank. The poles were generally six feet long. In the field, however, muskets were preferred.*

As commander of the Continental Army, General
Washington wears a pale blue sash across his body. His
uniform is basically the same he wore as captain
commanding the Fairfax County Independent Company, which
he first wore to take command of the Continental Army.
(Roffe/Osprey)

and New Jersey seem to have received a 'newly invented Napsack and haversack in one'. This consisted of a large piece of linen, folded into a pocket at either end. A leather strap, buckled in the centre, came out of the fold between the two pockets and was worn across the chest. The two sides were closed with three leather straps and buckles and a blanket seems to have been carried between the two. The outside pocket was painted red, while the inside pocket was left unpainted so that it could be washed.

Washing a haversack at first appealed to the soldier, who tossed his uncooked meat, gill of peas or beans, and butter unceremoniously into it. After only a short time, especially in the hot sun, the haversack became a smelly, greasy affair. The veterans, however, soon learned to ignore its appearance, and would reach into its dark interior and pluck out a piece of bread and eat it with apparent gusto.

Even poorly fed, ill-dressed, and badly equipped troops can fight well if they have good morale and weapons. The average infantryman went to war in 1775 with whatever musket he could bring from home. Sometimes this would be a fowling-piece, which would do double duty, first as a sporting and hunting gun, secondly as a weapon to carry on the annual militia days. Other times, the infantryman's weapon would be an old French or British musket left over from the previous war.

When war appeared on the verge of breaking out, the state committees of safety began issuing contracts for muskets, mostly copied closely from the British model. Congress, itself, set up the standard pattern in July 1775, when it,

'recommended to the several Assemblies or conventions of the colonies respectively, to set up and keep their gunsmiths at work, to manufacture good fire locks, with bayonets; each firelock to be made with a good bridle lock, $\frac{3}{4}$ of an inch bore, and of good substance at the breech, the barrel to be 3 feet 8 inches in length, the bayonet to be 18 inches in the blade, with a steel ramrod, the upper loop thereof to be trumpet mouthed. . . .'

Most colonies put out contracts for their muskets, but Virginia set up a state manufactory to make its own.

These, along with captured British weapons taken from local armouries, made up the Continental Army's initial stocks. They would not be enough to fight a major war, and the colonists turned to foreign countries for further musket supplies; France supplied the largest number, as she also supplied uniforms. The French muskets, because of their obvious advantages, soon replaced the British design as the standard American musket.

Originally there was great belief in the accuracy of

*The hunting-shirt was a comfortable and serviceable field dress as worn by this officer of the 3rd Continental Dragoons. His only badge of rank is his crimson silk sash, rarely worn by Continental officers. His helmet is boiled leather and decorated with horsehair (Roffe/Osprey)*

the Pennsylvania rifle, when pitted against troops carrying smoothbore Brown Besses, and in June 1775 Congress authorized ten rifle companies, six from Pennsylvania, and two each in Maryland and Virginia, which were to join the main Continental Army. The rifle turned out to be less of a 'miracle' weapon than at first thought.

Riflemen often tended to be quite undisciplined, and their weapon had several serious flaws. Loading it took three times longer than loading a musket, and no bayonet could be fixed on rifles. Riflemen were hard put to defend themselves against musketmen, even though pikes were to be issued to them in lieu of bayonets. Feelings against rifles grew in the Army. In the 2nd Pennsylvania Regiment's orderly book for 12 May 1778 it was recorded that General Anthony Wayne ordered his quartermasters to 'make a return of the number of Rifles in each Brigade, in order to Exchange them for an equal number of Muskets and Bayonets'. Some rifles saw use, nonetheless, throughout the war, and their owners created something of a legend for themselves.

Muskets were more important in winning the war than rifles. From New Orleans came Spanish weapons, which were commonly used by southern troops. The Illinois Regiment of the Virginia State Forces received Spanish muskets, bayonets and belts, and Spanish cartridge-boxes. The 0·69-calibre Spanish muskets were like French ones, with brass furniture similar to German models. Their cartridge-boxes were exceptionally modern, with tin liners instead of blocks to hold the cartridges, and a small pouch on the box's front to hold spare flints.

Field officers carried pistols, usually of British, American, French, or Spanish make, and swords. Company officers carried swords and spontoons throughout the war.

Captain Stephen Olney, 2nd Rhode Island Regiment, recalled fighting in the attack on Redoubt Number 10 at Yorktown:

'I had not less than six or eight bayonets pushed at me; I parried as well as I could with my espontoon, but they broke off the blade part, and their bayonets slid along the handle of my espontoon and scaled my fingers: one bayonet pierced my thigh, and another stabbed me in the abdomen just about the hip bone. One fellow fired at me and I thought his ball took effect in my arm; by the light of his gun (it was a night attack), I made a thrust with the remains of my espontoon, in order the injure the sight of his eyes; but as it happened, I only made a hard stroke in his forehead.'

Initially, sergeants carried halberds. This weapon was not as useful in combat as the spontoon and was rarely carried.

Another symbol of rank was the epaulette, which as the Army became better organized and uniformed, became the standard mark of officers and non-commissioned officers. Field-grade officers wore two, usually silver, epaulettes, while captains wore one on the right shoulder, and lieutenants, ensigns, and cornets wore one on the left. Sergeants, in 1779, were ordered to wear two worsted epaulettes, while corporals were to wear one on the right shoulder. Infantry non-commissioned officers were to wear white epaulettes, artillery yellow, and dragoons blue.

From a disorganized mob which had to depend on different-coloured cockades to tell its officers apart, to a tough, hard-fighting army had been a long haul. But the Continental Army had made it.

# 6

# The American Army 1784–1815

On 2 June 1784, its successful war over, the Continental Congress reduced its army to eighty enlisted men and several officers, the top ranking one being a captain. West Point, with its government stores, was to have a garrison of fifty-five men, while the rest were sent to Fort Pitt, Pennsylvania.

Americans might be tired of war and ready to build a peaceful nation, but not the Indians whose land was being constantly confiscated by white settlers. They swept from the north-west time and again, raiding and burning. Within the year Congress had to increase its army, this time to an infantry regiment consisting of eight infantry and two artillery companies. Both corps wore blue coats with red facings, like the old Continentals. Artillery coats had yellow buttons, while the infantrymen had white buttons.

The first two campaigns against the Indians went poorly, and in the early 1790s Anthony Wayne was named to command the Army. He organized the Army as a legion, made up of four sub-legions. Each sub-legion consisted of one rifle and two infantry battalions, one dragoon troop, and one artillery company. Uniforms were still blue faced red, but hats were now bearskin-crested round hats. The hats were decorated differently according to legion. The 1st Sub-legion wore white bindings, while the 2nd Sub-legion had red turbans; the 3rd, yellow turbans; and the 4th, green turbans.

At the time of the legion's formation, coats looked about the same as they had done, but collars had become the stand-up variety, instead of the flat, turn-down ones of the last war. Canteens were all bound in iron and usually stamped 'U.States'.

Otherwise, stocks, shirts, breeches, waistcoats, and shoes were almost identical to those worn by the Continentals.

The legion approach to army organization was dropped by Congress in 1797 and the army reorganized in regimental style. Four infantry regiments, a corps of artillerists and engineers, and two light dragoon companies were then ordered to be raised.

The next year Congress raised the number of companies in each regiment from eight to ten. A crisis with France in 1799 led to a further build-up of twelve infantry and one cavalry regiment. In 1802, however, following President Thomas Jefferson's election, the Army was again reduced and its cavalry eliminated.

The only good thing in the 1802 cutbacks was the creation of a corps of engineers, consisting of ten artillery and engineer cadets and seven engineer officers. They were assigned to the new United States Military Academy, at West Point, New York. The next year nineteen enlisted men were added to the corps, 'to aid in making experiments and for other purposes'.

The enlisted men were issued with blue coats with black velvet collars and cuffs and yellow false buttonholes on collars, cuffs, and breasts. Although they were supposed to receive felt shakos, it was a year before they could be procured.

America might be interested in reducing its army, but in Europe all the great powers were involved in the greatest war fought to that time. Both England and France were equally determined that American supplies should not reach their enemies, and adopted

*The General commanding the U.S. Army in 1799 wore a uniform very similar to that of the previous war. The collar was now a standing 'rise-and-fall' type, separated from the lapels. It was fashionable then to button the lapels across. The white plume marks the wearer as the Army's commander. His black boots are lined in red morocco and his spurs were gold-plated.*(Roffe/Osprey)

policies of searching and seizing American ships they thought bound for enemy ports. Jefferson attempted to respond by prohibiting all trade with foreign countries, and later with England and France. Such a policy, however, simply played into the struggling powers' hands, and hurt American shipping and trade.

At the same time, however, Jefferson did realize that the Army would have to be rebuilt, and in 1808 Congress authorized a regular army consisting of

*The privates of the Light Artillery Regiment were all mounted and considered themselves to be members of an élite corps. The District of Columbia also raised a militia light artillery company.* (Youens/Osprey)

*Staffs were quite small, compared to those of modern armies. The staff officer had, however, a distinctive uniform. Only the aide-de-camp, when going into action, was allowed to wear the crimson sash worn by all other army officers.* (Youens/Osprey)

*Various buttons of, from left, the 3rd Artillery and 1st Rifle Regiments, the militia (or general issue button), and the 1st Light Artillery and 9th Infantry Regiments.*
(Rebecca Katcher)

175 officers and 2,389 enlisted men. The men were to be enlisted with a $16 bounty and receive, after being discharged five years later, 160 acres of land and three months' pay. At the same time, Congress authorized the Regiment of Light Artillery. This regiment, considered the *élite* of the Army, was unlike regular artillery regiments in that every man was mounted and its companies could be sent from place to place on the battlefield much more quickly than artillery whose men plodded on foot alongside their guns.

While a 'glamorous' unit like the Light Artillery could usually find enough men to fill its ranks, the infantry could not. A private's pay was $5 a month and, in a developing country like the United States where the average unskilled labourer could earn at least $9 a month, very few people were interested in military careers. The Army got more than its share of British deserters from Canada and men on the run from the law.

Nor were the officers much better than their men. Until the founding of the Academy at West Point, all of them had either been appointed directly from civilian life, or had served as cadets with active,

*A typical militia knapsack, elaborately decorated.*
(Smithsonian Institution)

serving units. By 1812 the Academy had graduated eighty-nine men, out of whom only sixty-five were still serving in the Army.

The rate of drop-outs indicates a real problem in the American Army. Congressional policies, constantly enlarging and reducing the Army's size, had created a feeling among its most capable officers that there was no future in its ranks. Many of the more able men had gone back into private life. Those remaining were apt to be uneducated and, at best, indifferent officers. In 1811, for example, the captain commanding Fort Knox fled the territory after shooting and killing a subordinate officer.

When the Army was enlarged in 1808, a number of new officers was appointed, again without much specialized military training. Among them were Zachary Taylor and Winfield Scott, both of whom were to gain much later fame. Scott wrote that the officers in the old Army were 'very generally sunk into either sloth, ignorance, or habits of intemperate drinking', while officers of his group were 'coarse and ignorant men . . . swaggerers . . . decayed gentlemen, and others – "fit for nothing else", which always turned out utterly unfit for any purpose whatsoever'.

Not only were the officers of poor quality, but chances to learn what was necessary to run a large army in the field simply didn't exist. A tiny Regular Army, scattered about the country in posts with no more than sixty men each, was a poor school for that

*The 13th U.S. Infantry's national colour.* (West Point Collections, U.S. Military Academy)

sort of training. The Army's entire staff consisted of an adjutant-inspector-general, a paymaster, and an adjutant. The Army's senior officer, Brigadier-General James Wilkinson, had been away from Washington most of his service and had little voice in war planning.

*The 1st U.S. Infantry, of which this private is a member, served in the first campaigns around Detroit in 1812. (Youens/Osprey)*

Ready or not, war was looming on the horizon and the Army would be in the middle of it.

In January 1812, as war seemed likely at any moment, Congress authorized a Regular Army of 15,603 men. There were no more than 4,000 men in uniform at that time. In February, one-year enlistments for 30,000 more volunteers were allowed. By June the Army had reached a strength of 6,744 although only 5,087 were actually on duty.

On 4 June 1812 President James Madison asked Congress to declare war on England. The House of Representatives approved quickly, but the Senate did so only after much debate, on 18 June, and then only by six votes. A similar Senate proposal to declare war on France failed passage by only two votes.

The same feelings which divided Congress also divided the nation. New England states, which depended on trade with Canada and abroad, were generally against the war, while western and southern states were in favour of it. Still, with the actual declaration of war, more enthusiasm for joining the Army was shown.

That April, 15,000 eighteen-month additional enlistments were planned and men were coming out to join at a quicker pace. With so many out of work in the cities, due to the halting of foreign trade, the Army, especially for a short term, seemed not such a bad place to be. Pay had been raised to $10 a month, and enlistment bounties of $124 and 320 acres of land on discharge were authorized.

Never, however, was it easy to fill regular ranks. According to the Adjutant-General, 'although the numerical force in January, 1814 was 23,614, the actual strength of the army at that time was less than half that number, arising from the expiration of the term of service of the troops raised in 1809 and enlisted for five years, and of the twelve-and eighteen-months troops enlisted in 1812–1813'.

In the rapid call-up, the President was authorized to raise 30,000 Federal volunteers and seventeen companies of rangers. The latter were recruited largely in Ohio, Indiana, Illinois, and Kentucky. The *Army Register*, which first appeared 29 December 1813, listed enough officers of volunteer units for some twelve ranger companies, forty-six companies of United States Volunteers, and five companies of United States Sea Fencibles – coast defence troops in the Federal service, but distinguished from regulars by the fact that they were temporary units.

These officers, again, were often promoted to fill up the enlarged Army without much training. The Army's 'rules with regard to promotion' called for 'original vacancies' to be fialled by selection, while 'accidental vacancies' were made up by seniority.

*Privates of the 1st Company, 113th Pennsylvania Militia Regiment wore plain grey uniforms on their way to the battle of North Point in 1814. Their sergeant was marked by a red plume in his hat, while the musicians wore all-red uniforms. The company's commanding officer wore a blue coat with red collar and cuffs. (Youens/Osprey)*

Furthermore, 'Promotions to the rank of captain will be made *regimentally*; to that of field appointments by *line*, the light artillery, dragoons, artillery, infantry, and riflemen being kept always distinct.'

The same regulations which spelled out promotion procedures, the *Rules and Regulations of the Army of the United States*, which were first published 1 May 1813, also divided the country into nine military districts and assigned different regiments to recruit out of each one. The District of Columbia and its surrounding area later became the tenth district.

Two companies of light artillery, three troops of the 2nd Light Dragoons, one battalion of the 1st Artillery, and the 4th, 9th, and 21st Infantry Regiments would recruit in Massachusetts and New Hampshire. Rhode Island and Connecticut would provide men for one troop of the 2nd Light Dragoons, one battalion of the 1st Artillery, and the 25th Infantry. Two companies of light artillery, two troops of the 2nd Light Dragoons, two battalions of the 3rd Artillery and the 6th and 15th Infantry were to come from parts of New York and New Jersey. The rest of New Jersey, Pennsylvania, and Delaware would supply men for two companies of light artillery, two troops of the 2nd Light Dragoons, a battalion of the 2nd Artillery, and the 3rd, 5th, 16th, and 22nd Infantry. Two companies of light artillery, a troop of the 1st Light Dragoons, one and a half battalions of the 2nd Artillery, and the 12th, 14th, and 20th Infantry Regiments would be drawn from Maryland and Virginia.

Further south, both Carolina and Georgia were to send men into two troops of the 1st Light Dragoons, a battalion of the 1st Artillery, the 8th, 10th, and 18th Infantry. Two troops of the 1st Light Dragoons, a battalion of the 1st Artillery, and the 2nd, 7th, and 24th Infantry Regiments, and three companies of riflemen would be drawn from Louisiana, the Mississippi territory, and Tennessee.

Out west, Kentucky, Ohio, the Indiana territory, Michigan, Illinois, and Missouri were to send men into two companies of light artillery, three troops of the 1st Light Dragoons, one and a half battalions of the 2nd Artillery, the 1st, 17th, and 19th Infantry Regiments, and four rifle companies. Two troops of the 2nd Light Dragoons, two battalions of the 3rd Artillery, the 11th, 13th, and 23rd Infantry Regiments, and three rifle companies were to come from northern New York and Vermont.

*Ensign John Reese, 5th Maryland Infantry Regiment, wore this epaulette at the battle of North Point. (Fort McHenry National Monument and Historic Shrine)*

Later regiments were recruited where needed.

In addition, each state was to supply different quotas of its militia. All told, 100,000 militiamen were to be taken into Federal service from the fifteen states. The governors of Massachusetts, Connecticut, and Rhode Island, with 13,500 men between them, refused to obey this order, insisting that it was un-constitutional and therefore illegal. State militia need not, they argued, be made to serve outside their state borders. Generally, New Englanders approved their governors' moves.

New York's militia was organized in the typical manner. It had twenty-two militia regiments – twenty regular infantry, one light infantry, and one rifle regiment – arranged into two divisions with eight brigades. The first three and the seventh brigades consisted of three regiments each, while the fourth brigade had four regiments, and the fifth and sixth brigades were made up of two regiments. The light infantry and rifle regiments were posted to the eighth brigade.

Militia was a standing organization. Each American community had its own militia of all its able-bodied men between the ages of sixteen and sixty. Each man was to own his own musket and was required to serve in one or two annual musters. In terms of training and abilities, such actions did not produce the best possible types of units to have in battle. They were, none the less, the mainstay of any national defence efforts.

In case of the state's invasion, the militia was to be uniformed and placed on virtually the same basis as the regulars. The Pennsylvania General Assembly, typical of most states, prescribed uniforms quite similar to the regulars:

'Infantry and Light Infantry and Cavalry of the militia to wear blue coats faced with red and with white linings, white pantaloons; Artillery to wear blue coats faced with red with red linings, blue pantaloons. Infantry and Light Infantry metal, white; Cavalry and Artillery brass. Hats to be round, black, brims not more than 3 inches; red and blue cockades.

'Grey coats and pantaloons to be worn when blue coats and white or blue pantaloons are not available. Hunting shirts and overalls to be optional summer wear.

'Regimental colours to be dark blue: in the centre an eagle displayed, in his right talon an olive branch and in his left a sheath of arrows, bearing on his breast the State escutcheon; in the upper corner nearest the staff a circle of thirteen white stars enclosing the regimental numeral and the letters "PA." The colours to be six feet six inches in the fly and four feet six inches on the staff; the lance to be nine feet

*The shako worn by Ensign Reese. The cords are white, the plate silver.* (Fort McHenry National Monument and Historic Shrine)

At the same time, however, the men's dress failed to match their magnificent colours. Said a New Orleans man who saw them when they marched to the defence of that city:

'Their appearance was not very military. In their woolen hunting shirts and copperas dyed pantaloons; with slouched hats made from the skins of racoons or foxes, with belts of untanned deer-skin in which were stuck their hunting knives and tomahawks – with their long unkempt hair and unshorn faces . . . but (they) were admirable soldiers remarkable for endurance and possessing that admirable quality in soldiers of being able to care of themselves.'

Besides the mass of militia, and much more dependable than it, there were hundreds of independent volunteer companies. These bore such splendid

long surmounted by a spear point six inches long. The State Colour to be seven red and six white stripes in a dark blue canton repeating the same device as the Regimental Colour; dimensions of the State Colour and its lance to be the same as for the Regimental Colour.'

Other state regiments might have even more fanciful colours. The Tennessee Militia under Brigadier-General Andrew Jackson carried a national flag made of silk, while their second colour was made of white satin. It was embroidered with, from the top, eighteen stars on organdie, two sprigs of laurel lying athwart, then the words, 'Tennessee Volunteers – Independence, in a state of war, is to be maintained on the battle-ground of the Republic. The tented field is the post of honour. Presented by the Ladies of East Tennessee, Knoxville, February, 10th, 1813.' Below this was a display of the implements of war. The colour's wings were dove-colour lutestring, ornamented with white fringe and tassels.

Perhaps they thought the enemy would be so interested in trying to read this elaborate colour, the Tennessee men could move up almost unnoticed.

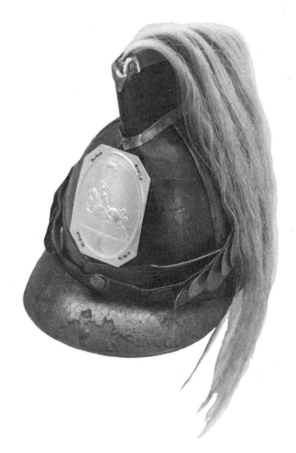

*The regulation leather dragoon helmet.* (Fort McHenry National Monument and Historic Shrine)

names as the four companies which defended St Michaels on 10 August 1813: the Easton Fencibles, Mechanic Volunteers, Hearts of Oak, and Independent Volunteers. They were usually beautifully clad in uniforms of their own design – they often voted on them – and up to the top standards of the drill field. Usually they drilled weekly, in the evenings, and often held parades. They were, in reality, the heart of any local defence.

Even with the fancy dress and frequent meetings, however, the volunteer companies were simply not up to the quality of regulars. They may have called themselves, 'Hearts of Oak', or more typical military names, but, as District of Columbia Militia Major of Brigade John S. Williams wrote:

'. . . as a cowl does not make a monk, to dress and equip a body of men as light infantry or dragoons does not make them what they are called. They must be disciplined and have some experience in the peculiar duties, before they are entitled to the name.

'A company of cavalry, formed in the heart of a large commercial city, might choose to assume the name of "Cossacks" and provide themselves with lances and other suitable equipments, but they would remain, in reality, just what they were before – a parcel of inoffensive clerks or journeymen mechanics.'

'Inoffensive clerks' or not, when the enemy appeared, they were needed. Such was the case in August 1814 when Captain James H. Rogers sent out the following typical order to his company of the 51st Maryland Militia Regiment:

'Sir, In obedience to a Regimental Order, you will furnish yourself with a Knapsack, Canteen and Ten rounds ball Cartridges, suitable to your Firelock, and hold yourself in readiness to repair immediately to my quarters on the George Town Road, with arms and accoutrements, upon any Alarm that may be given, by the ringing of the watch bell. Our Enemy is at the door, therefore it is hoped that no Man, who wishes well to his Country, will be missing.'

When that alarm was given, it was a great adventure to go off to war. Private John Pendleton Kennedy, of the 5th Maryland Regiment, marched off with his regiment to the smashing defeat at Bladensburg.

*The plain white linen hunting-shirt of the previous war had become a symbol of American marksmanship and was widely worn in the War of 1812. Maryland riflemen, like this one, used red fringe, although most others were fringed yellow. (Youens/Osprey)*

'It was a day of glorious anticipation that Sunday morning when, with all the glitter of a dress parade, we set forth on our march. As we moved through the streets the pavements were crowded with anxious spectators; the windows were filled with women; friends were rushing to the ranks to bid us goodbye – many exhorting us to be of good cheer and do our

*A leather cockade for an officer's* chapeau-de-bras. (Smithsonian Institution)

*The 2nd U.S. Dragoons saw much active service along the Canadian-U.S. border. The lieutenant-colonel's helmet is made of boiled leather, hard as iron. The issue cap-plate was of pewter, although officers often had silver ones. The same basic uniform was worn by all ranks.* (Roffe/Osprey)

duty; handkerchiefs were waving from the fair hands at the windows – some few of the softer sex weeping as they waved adieux to husbands and brothers; the populace were cheering and huzzahing at every corner as we hurried along in brisk step to familiar music, with banners fluttering in the wind and bayonets flashing in the sun.

'What a scene it was, and what a proud actor I was in it! I was in the ecstasy of a vision of glory, stuffed with any quantity of romance. This was a real army marching to a real war. The enemy, we knew, was in full career and we had the certainty of meeting him in a few days.

'Unlike our customary parades, our march now had all the equipments of a campaign. Our wagon-train was on the road; our cartridge-boxes were filled; we had our crowd of camp servants and followers. Officers rode backward and forward along the flanks of the column with a peculiar gallop – the invariable form in which military conceit shows itself in the first movements towards a campaign. The young officers wish to attract attention, and so seem to be always on the most important messages.

'As for me – not yet nineteen – I was too full of the exultation of the time to think of myself – all my fervor was spent in admiration of this glittering army. I thought of these verses and they spoke of my delight.

It were worth ten years of peaceful life
One glance at their array.'

Private Kennedy described his uniform and equipment as well:

'We were in winter cloth uniform, with a most absurd helmet of thick jacked leather and covered with plumes. We carried, besides, a knapsack in which – in my own case – I had packed the great-coat, my newly acquired blanket, two or three shirts, stockings, etc.

'Among these articles I had also put a pair of pumps which I had provided with the idea that, after we had beaten the British army and saved Washington, Mr. Madison would very likely invite us to a ball at the President's House, and I wanted to be ready for it.'

With this knapsack, weighing, he figured, ten pounds, and his 'fourteen-pound' Harper's Ferry musket, he was carrying quite a load:

'Take our burden altogether and we could not have been tramping over those sandy roads, under the broiling sun of August, with less than thirty pounds of weight upon us. But we bore it splendidly, toiling and sweating in a dense cloud of dust, drinking the muddy water of the little brooks which our passage over them disturbed, and taking all the discomforts with a cheerful heart and a stout resolve.'

*Two views of Captain John Wool's coat, 13th U.S. Infantry* (Rensselaer County Historical Society)

*The 2nd Artillery's shako-plate was of a regimental design, unique to it.* (Rebecca Katcher)

Not that militiamen always had such stout resolve. At the battle of Queenston Heights the New York militiamen refused to cross the river and reinforce the 6th and 13th Infantry Regiments, then under heavy British attack. They stood about on the American side of the river, engaging the regular officers with arguments about whether it was constitutional for militiamen to be ordered outside their own states.

This behaviour was typical of militiamen on the invasions of Canada. It was the Regular Army which would have to do that job.

Not that the American regulars, quickly made into a brand-new army, were that much superior to militia or volunteers in the martial arts. Colonel Roger Purdy, 4th Infantry, wrote of Brigadier-General Wade Hampton's force of regulars that it,

and if taken into action in their present state, will prove more dangerous to themselves than to their enemy.'

One cause of the poor quality of troops was, of course, the equally poor quality of officers. The Baltimore newspaper, *Nile's Weekly Register*, reported to its readers, 'with great pleasure', on 14 August 1813, that,

'gen. Hampton is busily employed in making *soldiers* of the *officers* of the army at *Burlington*. They are frequently and severly drilled; and given to understand that they must and shall ascertain and perform their several duties. This is striking at the very root of our disasters. The best materials for an army that the world could furnish, have been sacrificed to the pompous ignorance or inconsiderable courage of those who should have applied them to victory.'

Once officers had learned their duties, they could begin to train their men. Major Jessup, commanding the 25th Infantry, wrote that 'he began, under the

*Note the collar decoration on General Andrew Jackson's coat.* (Smithsonian Institution)

'consisting of about 4,000 men, was composed principally of recruits who had been but a short time in the service, and had not been exercised with that rigid discipline so essentially necessary to constitute the soldier. They had indeed been taught various evolutions, but a spirit of subordination was foreign to their views.'

An inspecting officer's report on the 14th Infantry in 1812, soon to lose its regimental colours to the 49th Regiment of Foot, probably summed up the entire American Army so quickly converted from civilians to soldiers: 'The 14th is composed entirely of recruits; they appear to be almost as ignorant of their duty as if they had never seen a camp, and scarcely know on which shoulder to carry the musket. They are mere militia, and, if possible, even worse;

orders of General Scott, a course of instruction, and kept his command under arms from seven to ten hours a day. A similar course was pursued by the chiefs of the other corps. The consequence was, that when we took the field in July our corps manœuvred in action and under the fire of the enemy's artillery with the accuracy of parade.'

*The artillery kept their long skirts on their coats, although they could not obtain the ordered* chapeau-de-bras *hats. The sergeant is marked by his epaulettes, sash, and sword.* (Youens/Osprey)

One thing the new regimental members would have to learn was the formation of their regiment in line of battle. In action, the troops were arranged in order of regimental seniority, with the senior regiments on the right. Each regiment was made up of eight battalion and two light infantry companies.

The battalion companies were divided into half-battalions, called left and right wings. The first, third, fifth, and seventh battalion companies were on the right, the rest on the left. The two light companies were posted on the battalion's right, by their captain's seniority.

Each company was divided into two platoons, which were again divided into two sections.

In action, the battalion was drawn up in two lines. Exact battle tactics were generally given just before the campaign or battle, but those of General Smyth as given to Lieutenant-Colonel Winder, 14th Infantry are typical:

'1. The artillery will spend some of their first shot on the enemy's artillery, and then aim at the infantry, raking them where it is practicable. 2. The firing of musketry by wings or companies will begin at the distance of two hundred yards, aiming at the middle and firing deliberately. 3. At twenty yards' distance the soldiers will be ordered to trail arms, advance with shouts, fire at five paces' distance and charge bayonets. 4. The soldiers will be silent, above all things, attentive at the word of command, load quick and well and aim low.'

Even with the training and experience, there was still a healthy feeling of respect for an enemy which had fought so many battles against the best troops Europe had to offer. In the night battle outside New Orleans Lieutenant Colonel Ross, commanding the 7th and 44th Infantry Regiments, held his men back from hand-to-hand combat with the British, feeling they would have little chance crossing cold steel with British regulars.

The British were more than simply the enemy; in fact, they were in many ways the model on which the Americans based their army. The American uniform was a prime example. After using the round hats, infantry platoon officers and enlisted men were ordered in late 1811 into black cylindrical caps of felt or beaver copied from the British shakos. These were $6\frac{7}{8}$ to $7\frac{1}{4}$ in. tall, with a $2\frac{1}{2}$ in. visor, cord and tassels, and a front plate 'with the eagle, the number of the regiment and designation of the service'.

Dragoons, in 1808, were to wear 'leather Caps or Helmets, with blue Feathers, tipt with White . . . the feathers of privates not to exceed ten inches in length'. A strip of bearskin was attached to the top, with the letters 'USLD' in brass on front. A few years later the cap was changed and a front plate, instead of the letters, was issued. According to the 1812 Regulations, dragoons were to wear a 'Helmet, according to pattern, blue feather with white top, feather 9 inches long'.

The artillery was to wear a full *chapeau bras*, quite a large beaver or felt hat, made like the old tricornes with only two ends and a large cockade on front. Unfortunately, or fortunately if you had to wear one of the things, contractors failed to supply these hats to the 2nd and 3rd Artillery Regiments – in fact, it was impossible to get anybody to make them. The two regiments, therefore, were allowed to draw light artillery shakos, like infantry ones, with different-style brass shako plates.

The coat, also, was basically the same as the British one. It was made of heavy wool, again with unhemmed edges. It had short tails, lined in white wool, although there was no lining in the coat's body. The coat was blue with red collar and cuffs, the collar reaching almost to the ear-lobe. The sleeves were quite long, the Commissary-General being told in 1814 that 'The sleeve of a jacket, being cut to come to the knuckle, after wetting will shrink nearly to the wristbone.' Infantry coats were trimmed with white wool worsted tape across the chest, on the collar, and on the cuffs.

Artillery coats were originally lapelled and fastened with hooks and eyes, but in August 1812 they were ordered to 'button from the chin'. They were trimmed in yellow worsted tape, and had long, old-fashioned tails. Each artillery enlisted man's coat required eighteen yards of yellow tape and fifty brass buttons.

Trousers were wool gaitered trousers, officially grey, but also seen in brown and green. Officers' trousers were blue wool and generally tucked into boots.

Dragoons received dress braided hussar coats with three rows of ball buttons and single-breasted blue fatigue jackets. For dress they had braided white cassimere or buckskin pantaloons, and for fatigue, blue wool.

Non-commissioned officers wore the same coats as privates. Infantry corporals wore one white worsted fringed epaulette on their right shoulders, while artillery corporals had yellow epaulettes. Sergeants had two white or yellow epaulettes, depending on their corps. In addition, sergeants wore scarlet wool worsted sashes and carried straight swords.

*The 1st Rifle Regiment began the war in 'bottle-green' coats. In 1814, when the 2nd, 3rd, and 4th Rifle Regiments were authorized, the uniforms were changed to grey. Men of the 1st managed to keep their old green ones as long as they could. (Youens/Osprey)*

Infantry sergeants' swords had iron hilts, while those of artillery sergeants were brass-hilted.

Officers wore similar coats, rather plain, only their red collars being set off by silver lace for infantry, gold for artillery. They carried brass-hilted swords and wore crimson silk sashes. A subaltern wore a silver or gold epaulette on his left shoulder; a captain, the same on the right shoulder, and field officers on both shoulders. Officers, posted in places so far from headquarters, often made minor changes in the uniform to suit themselves, wearing fancy swords or shako plates.

Cavalrymen carried iron-hilted sabres in japan-ned black scabbards carried in buff waistbelts. Their pistols were brass-mounted, and were carried in holsters on either side of their saddle-fronts. They carried carbines for fighting when dismounted.

An infantryman carried on his right hip, suspended by a whitened buff leather belt, a black leather cartridge-box, 'with blocks bored for 26 cartridges of ball nineteen to the pound of stout leather, having under the block a tin container of three compartments for 6 cartridges to be in each end compartment and for flints and oil rags in the middle one. To this a little leather pocket in front of the box affords admittance.'

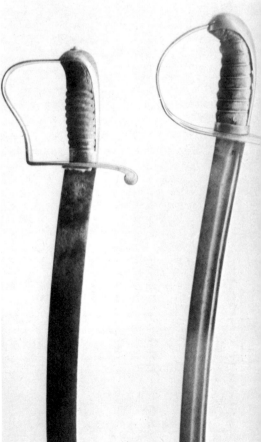

*The ivory and brass artillery officer's sword-hilt. Its metal scabbard is also shown.* (Smithsonian Institution)

*Two types of iron-mounted cavalry sabres.* (Smithsonian Institution)

On his left side hung his brass-tipped bayonet-scabbard, hooked on to a whitened buff belt with a plain pewter oval belt-plate in front. The iron bayonet had a 16-inch triangular-shaped blade. Over that hung a linen haversack, generally water-proofed by painting, and a light blue painted, iron-bound wooden canteen. Usually his regimental designation was painted on its side in red or white.

His knapsack was also painted blue, usually with a large red 'U.S.' in the centre, and he carried his grey blanket and greatcoat folded inside.

Another infantry-type organization was the rifle regiment. In 1812 there had been only the single Regiment of Riflemen, but in 1814 the 2nd, 3rd, and 4th Regiments of Riflemen were added to the Army's rolls. Originally riflemen had been dressed in green coats faced black in winter, and fringed green linen hunting-shirts in summer. In February 1812 their uniform description was sent to the Purveyor of Public Supplies:

'Dress of the Head: Field officers will wear the *chapeaux bras* bound with black; the buttons, tassel loops & eagle yellow, the plume green. The company officers will wear black caps like those of the infantry, the band, tassels, & eagles yellow, the plume green.

'Uniforms: The skirts of the coats of the officers will be long; those of Company officers short, the colour of the coat bottle green. The collar trimmed with gold lace all round, two lace holes on each side; plain Breast herring bone buttonholes of twist; four buttons and as many blind buttonholes of Twist on each cuff; the buttons yellow (actually they were made of copper) stamped with eagles and the letter R on the shield. The vest white; the pantaloons bottle green, in the summer white.

'The uniform of non-commissioned officers and soldiers will resemble that of the company officers. The collars and cuffs to be black, the pocket flaps across the skirt indented below, with four buttons and twist holes, the buttons or cuffs across. The undress coat shall have the cape and cuffs of the same colour with the coat. Field officers cloaks to be of bottle green with a standing collar of the same lined with black. Black stocks.'

Officers and non-commissioned officers seem to have carried the same side-arms as the infantry,

*The 1st Rifle Regiment's brass shako-plate.* (Rebecca Katcher)

although sergeants' swords were probably brass-hilted.

While the riflemen had their hunting-shirts for lightweight summer dress, the rest of the Army was in need of summer garb. Originally the men had been expected to wear their white woollen long-sleeved waistcoats with their white linen gaitered trousers for summer. Unfortunately, this meant that the waistcoat, which had to be worn all winter, saw service all year long. A new piece of clothing had, therefore, to be issued.

In 1802 the Purveyor of Public Supplies issued a short, single-breasted linen coatee to all troops south of the Potomac River. These skirtless, long-sleeved coatees, closed with nine buttons in front, proved a success and were then issued to all troops but riflemen. When the Army was suddenly enlarged in 1812, these coatees came into use to supply the large numbers suddenly recruited and appeared in the north as well as the south. By 1814, however, supplies were fairly well available to the whole Army and the coatees were once again restricted in use to the south.

The nicely designed wool coatees, with different facings, became impossible to provide in a country as little industrialized as the United States, anyway. In 1813, therefore, a new uniform was ordered.

In March 1813 the Commissary-General wrote to the Secretary of War to say that everyone would be pleased with 'a plain blue coatee, without a particle of red to it, with white or buff cross belts, white vests & white overalls with gaiters for Infantry & Artillery. . . . The coats should be single breasted, to button from the collar to the waist.' Accordingly, orders appeared stating that:

'The coat of the infantry and artillery shall be uniformly blue; no red collars or cuffs; and no lace shall be worn by any grade, excepting in epaulettes and sword knots.

'All officers will wear coats of the length of those worn by field officers: all the rank and file will wear coatees. The button holes of these will be trimmed with tape on the collar only. Leather caps will be substituted for felt, and worsted or cotton pompons for feathers.

'General officers, and all others of the general staff, not otherwise directed, shall wear cocked hats without feathers, gilt bullet buttons, and button holes in the *herring-bone* form.

'The epaulettes of Major Generals will have on the gold ground of each strap, two silvered stars.

'The epaulettes of Brigadiers will have on each strap one star.

'The uniform of the Physician and Surgeon, and Apothecary Generals, and Hospital Surgeons and Mates, shall be black, the coats with standing collars, and on each side of the collar, a star of embroidery, within half an inch of the front edge.

*The 1813-pattern leather shako, with an officer's non-regulation silver plate on front. The cords, plume, and cockade are missing.* (Smithsonian Institution)

*From these fortifications Andrew Jackson's men fought the battle of New Orleans. Two men wear reconstructed summer-issue linen uniforms.* (Melville Cohen IV)

'The rules with respect to undress, are dispensed with, excepting that cockades must always be worn.'

The leather caps were especially desired. The Commissary-General of Purchases had previously written that

'For the men of the Light Artillery, Infantry, Artillery and Rifle Regiments. I propose to furnish Leather Caps in lieu of Felt Caps, the former being preferable as to appearance, comfort, durability and on the score of economy, the leather cap will cost $1. The Felt Cap costs 87½ Cts. the former will last three to four years with decency, under any circumstances two years, the latter but one year and will not look decent half that time, the first wetting injures its good appearance. . . .'

The new shako had its plume on the left and a cord from the bottom of the left to the top of the right, from where hung two tassels. A separate piece of thin leather was sewn in the back, to be let down for protection in the rain. It had a false front, like the new British shako of which it was a copy, rising almost three inches above the crown. The rest of the dimensions were about the same as those of the felt cap.

Waistcoats were still white, single breasted, without pocket-flaps. Officers were now to wear blue pantaloons in the winter and white nankeen in the summer. Their coat-tails were decorated with a blue cloth diamond at each false turnback.

Musicians – fifers and drummers in foot regiments and buglers in mounted – were still to wear scarlet wool coats. Before, however, their collars and cuffs were blue; under these new regulations their coats were all scarlet.

Riflemen were also bothered with the problems of procuring cloth. Besides getting their leather caps, they were issued with grey wool coats instead of green, as green wool was impossible to buy. The 1st Regiment, which still had green coats in stores, kept the old colour as long as it could, but, eventually, even it had to join the drab 2nd, 3rd, and 4th Rifle Regiments in wearing grey.

They were not the only troops to be put into grey uniforms. On the Niagara frontier in 1814 General Scott requested new uniforms for his 1st Brigade, made up of the 9th, 11th, 22nd, and 25th Infantry Regiments. The Quartermaster in Philadelphia

told him that, regretfully, there was no blue cloth in stores. Would he mind if they received coatees made of grey wool? Scott was much more concerned in getting his troops in shape to fight than for a parade, and accepted the grey. Much, it may be

*Men of the 9th, 11th, 22nd, and 25th U.S. Infantry Regiments in 1813 were issued with grey coats instead of blue because of the shortage of blue cloth in the United States. The men were unhappy about this, grey being generally used by labourers and slaves. However, after their performances at Chippewa and Lundy's Lane, the U.S. Military Academy adopted it for their cadet uniforms in their honour. (Youens/Osprey)*

added, to the men's disgust. Grey wool was generally worn only by common labourers and slaves.

Regiments through late 1812 to early 1813 usually received other than blue coats, although they tried to keep the colours uniform in each regiment. In this period, coats for the different regiments were: 8th, black and brown; 10th, blue and brown; 12th, drab; 14th, drab and brown; 15th, grey or mixed; 16th, black; 17th, blue, brown, drab and black; 18th, blue; 20th drab and brown, and 22nd, drab.

It was not only wool that was hard to come by. In the winter of 1812 clothing ordered in September for the 17th, 19th, and 24th Infantry Regiments failed to arrive in the north-west, and local women made up 1,800 heavy shirts for them. Even shoes were lacking, and only in December were they generally available.

Regulars of the 17th Infantry were described as wearing badly worn-out linen summer fatigue coatees at the battle of Frenchtown, Michigan, 18 January 1813. Along with the regulars were men of the 1st and 5th Kentucky Regiments and the Kentucky Rifle Regiment. They were all in quite a bad way, as Major John Richardson, a British eye-witness of the battle, noted.

'Their appearance was miserable to the last degree. They had the air of men to whom cleanliness was a virtue unknown, and their squalid bodies were covered by habiliments that had evidently undergone every change of season and were arrived at the last stage of repair. . . . It was the depth of winter; but scarcely an individual was in possession of a great coat or cloak, and few of them wore garments of wool of any description. They still retained their summer dress, consisting of cotton stuff of various colours shaped into frocks and descending to the knee. Their trousers were of the same material. They were covered by slouch hats, worn bare by constant use, beneath which their long hair fell matted and uncombed over their cheeks; and

*Captain Benjamin Burch led the District of Columbia's light artillery militia wearing these wings.* (Smithsonian Institution)

these, together with the dirty blankets wrapped round their loins to protect them against the inclemency of the season, and fastened with broad leathern belts, into which were thrust axes and knives of enormous length, gave them an air of wilderness and savageness which in Italy would cause them to pass for brigands of the Appenines. The only distinction between the garb of the officer, and that of the soldier was that the one, in addition to his sword, carried a short rifle instead of a long one, while a dagger, often curiously worked and of some value, supplied the place of the knife.'

Not that all the men at Frenchtown were without any finery. Captain Hart, formerly of the Lexington Light Infantry, was described as wearing a crimson silk sash.

In the south, too, uniforms were hard to obtain. A British Royal Artillery officer, Benson Earle Hill, described meeting a soldier, probably a member of Beale's Rifles, near New Orleans:

'I had observed, upon two or three occasions, when I had to pass a part of our cantonement devoted to the prisoners taken on the night of the 23rd, one who appeared absorbed in melancholy, and whose manner and bearing betokened him of superior rank to his fellows. . . . he, as well as many others, was dressed in a most unsoldier-like and fantastic costume. It consisted of a tunic reaching to the knee, with a large cape covering the shoulder; the whole made of blue and white check, the edges trimmed with short white fringe.

'I could not resist inquiring of my newly-made acquaintence the origin of this singular uniform, and learnt that the check was the only commodity the city afforded in sufficient quantity to clothe the corps to which he belonged, consisting solely of Americans. They were anxious, for reasons of their own, to be distinguished from the French and Spanish settlers of New Orleans. They were armed with rifles, and had suffered severely in the night attack.'

Yet another rifleman presented a different picture:

'I perceived a tall figure approaching me, whose appearance I think it worthy of description. He was a young man, of about two or three and twenty,

*A black wooden canteen with red trim.* (Smithsonian Institution)

good looking but pale from a recent wound, indicated by his arm being tied up in a pocket-hankerchief . . . he wore a high conically-shaped hat. . . . His dress consisted of a coarse reddish-brown cloth coat, with huge metal buttons, a waistcoat of deer skin, and trowsers of thick dreadnought . . . with a strong nasal twang, (he) thus addressed me: . . . "I was raised in old Kentuck . . . found myself wounded and taken prisoner, what hell fire luck my brother Bob had in stopping at home, although he was appointed ensine to our company of Rifles. . . ." '

The rifle may have not been a terribly efficient weapon in the last war, but it had been shown to have some uses. In 1792 the Army had made its first purchase of rifles, enough to arm a 325-strong battalion. When the 1st Rifle Regiment was authorized, the job of arming them was given to the Harper's Ferry, Virginia, arsenal. Arsenal gunsmiths designed a weapon based on the Pennsylvania rifle, the Model 1803. It was 0·54 calibre, firing a round ball weighing half an ounce. It used some seventy-five grains of powder in the charge, the ball being about half the weight of the musket ball.

The barrel was usually some thirty-three inches long, although they differed from each other since they were individually made. The barrel and underside rib, which held two ramrod sockets, were held to the walnut stock by a transverse sliding key. Unlike most military weapons, the stock was only twenty-six inches long, about half the weapon's length. It had a deep, crescent-shaped butt-plate, a good-sized brass patch-box on the butt's right side and a brass trigger-guard and skeleton pistol grip.

This remained the standard issue rifle, both for regulars and militia, until the 2nd, 3rd, and 4th Rifle Regiments were raised. Again, because of a shortage of supplies, a new, similar rifle was issued, with a barrel three inches shorter.

Militia units like Beale's Rifle Company were usually made up of men who owned their own rifles and used them in action. Every type of Pennsylvania rifle, made in virtually every state, was used by them. Men who owned their own rifles, too, were often pretty deadly with them. Every member of Beale's was reputed to be able to shoot the eye out of a squirrel at 100 paces. The paces may have been quite short, or the eye quite large, but undoubtedly the riflemen were good shots.

Even their rough garb may not have been that much of a disservice to them. Major Richardson, of the British Army, wrote after an ambush on the Canadian border in 1812:

'Here it was that we first had an opportunity of perceiving the extreme disadvantage of opposing regular troops to the enemy in the woods. Accustomed to the use of the rifle from his infancy – dwelling in a measure amid forests with the intricacies of which he is wholly acquainted, and possessing the advantages of a dress which renders him almost indistinguishable to the eye of a European, the American marksman enters with comparative security into a contest with the English soldier whose glaring habiliment and accoutrements are objects too conspicuous to be missed, while his utter ignorance of a mode of warfare, in which courage and discipline are of no avail, renders the struggle for mastery even more unequal. The . . . levies of men taken from the forests of Ohio (are) scarcely inferiour as riflemen to the Indians. Dressed in woollen frocks of a grey colour, and trained to cover their bodies behind the trees from which they fired, without exposing more of their persons than was absolutely necessary for their aim, they afforded us, on more than one occasion, the most convincing proofs that without the assistance of the Indian Warriors, the defence of so great a portion of Western Canada . . . would have proved a duty of great difficulty and doubt.'

This would have been true even if all Canadians had been loyal. They were not. The commander of the American forces at Sandwich, Canada, in 1812 had a number of offers to raise Canadian troops for American service. He did authorize a Simon Z. Watson to raise a Canadian cavalry unit for him.

*Many militia companies, like the Volunteer Rifles of New Orleans, were as much a social organization as a military one. This company was composed of sons of the best Creole families in that city, and their blue frocks are useful for hunting rather than showy.*

The most famous, or infamous, depending on how you look at it, unit raised from among the Canadians was the Canadian Volunteers. It was raised by Lieutenant-Colonel Joseph Willcocks, a member of the Upper Canada Legislative Assembly, in the spring of 1813. With a top strength of some seventy men, it was most famous for the burning of Newark and raids on Port Dover. During the latter raid it was led by another Canadian legislator, Major Abraham Markle.

The Canadian Volunteers were dressed and armed the same as the rest of the American troops. As with the American rifle, the American musket, which they received, was an excellent weapon.

It was in 1794 that Congress authorized the procurement of 7,000 new muskets and the establishment of two armouries. Harper's Ferry and Springfield, Massachusetts. Harper's Ferry became noted for both muskets and rifles, while the Springfield Armoury became the main supplier of American muskets.

Following the last war, the 1763-pattern French musket was made the standard American model. It was this weapon which was first produced in Springfield in 1795.

The Model 1795 musket was a typical flintlock with a 0.69-calibre bore. It was some five feet long, with a 44.75-in. barrel. All the metal parts were highly polished iron. The barrel was held to the walnut stock by three bands, the top one being notched to expose the barrel, and all three serving to hold the ramrod in place under the stock. In 1808 the hammer was changed by removing the ornamental curling at the top and the pan was now made as part of the lock-plate.

In 1812, seeing how different all the muskets had been made by private contractors and government armouries, the Ordnance Department decided to standardize all weapons. They selected a master model and required all their suppliers, both government and non-government, to adhere strictly to that pattern.

The suppliers, however, were allowed to use up all their old components first and therefore it wasn't until after the war that weapons began to take any really standard form. Still, the American musket, like the French one, was lighter; fired a lighter ball, meaning more could be easily carried; and was easier to care for with its barrel-bands instead of pins like the Brown Bess. It was an excellent weapon.

And it was in the hands of an army which had grown considerably, matured, and begun to take a philosophy and direction all of its own since those days when George Washington rode up the dusty roads to find the assembled mob acting as the 'armies of the United Colonies' back in 1775.

# 7 The British Army 1784–1815

The British Army which had taken a beating in the last war was not in the best of condition. According to one expert, the Army in 1793 was 'lax in its discipline, entirely without system and very weak in numbers. Each colonel of a regiment managed it according to his own notions, or neglected it altogether. There was no uniformity of drill or movement; professional pride was rare; professional knowledge still more so.' The Army, even in terms of numbers, was in a poor position to wage a major war. In 1782 there had been over 150,000 men in the Army – in 1793 this had dropped to 97,000, including both the English and Irish Establishments, infantry, cavalry, artillery, militia fencibles, and 35,000 troops from Hanover and Hesse. There were only 31,000 regular cavalry and infantrymen, in eighty-one battalions, throughout the world.

Still, lessons had been learned from the last war. One of the most important was the continued success of light infantry. The light companies were made regular battalion companies immediately after the war, but when war with the French began in 1793, they were reverted to light ones. More importantly, reaching back to the concept of the 80th Regiment of Light Armed Foot, Sir John Moore was sent to Shorncliffe to train a whole light brigade. He rationalized much of the harsh discipline, weeded out inefficient officers, and stressed musketry training. He taught himself to load and fire a musket five times a minute – instead of the old three and a half – and brought his brigade to that level of efficiency.

The musket they used, while basically similar to the last war's Brown Bess, was again slightly changed. As the war with France grew in scope, and thousands of men had to be armed, production of the relatively elaborate Short Land Model fell below what was necessary. The government then turned to the pattern of musket used by the East India Company and from 1797 gunsmiths were ordered to supply India Pattern muskets exclusively.

The India Pattern was still a 0·75-calibre musket, but with a 39-in. barrel. The number of ramrod-pipes had been reduced from four to three. The wrist escutcheon-plate was done away with. The side-plate lost its little tail behind the rear lock screw. The trigger-guard's finials were simplified and the reverse curl within the bow left off. The stock was made of an inferior heart and sap grade of walnut. Even more importantly, requirements for viewing and proof were made much less demanding.

Learning from the French muskets, the goose-necked cock, apt to be easily broken, was replaced by a reinforced one in 1809.

The Light Division, the name under which it became famous in the Peninsular campaign, was made up of the 43rd, 52nd, and 95th Regiments of Foot. Their exploits in that campaign, along with the equally famous exploits of virtually every regiment in the Army, totally revived the British soldier's faith in himself and the Army. When America declared war in 1812, the Army was ready for its job.

Light infantry, again, was among the troops sent. Not as a division for the American campaign, but in regiments.

The 43rd (Monmouthshire) Light Infantry saw

duty at the unsuccessful battle of New Orleans. They wore a felt, 8-in. tall hat known as the 'stove-pipe'. It was decorated with a green woollen tuft worn on its front, over a small brass bugle horn and green cords. Officers still had true scarlet coats, while the men's were dull brick-red. Facings were white in the 43rd.

Dress during this whole period changed roughly as the dress in the American Army. The tricornes of the Revolution became the bicorns, with a tall front and back, of the 1790s. In 1800 the stovepipe became the issue cap, with a bugle for light infantry and elaborate brass front-plates for the rest of the Army.

Towards the end of the 1780s the collar, which had been a flat, turn-down one, was made to stand taller and away from the lapel. In the 1790s this gave way to a simple standing collar. In 1785 shoulder-tabs of a facing colour, with regimental lace sewn around their edges, were ordered for all coats. The coats themselves were cut shorter than before. In 1797 all ranks were ordered to button their coats across their chests and, for the first time, waistcoats were hidden. That same year, lapels were done away with altogether and only the collar and cuffs were made in facing colours.

By the time war was actually declared in 1812, coats were single-breasted with the shoulder-tabs, collars, and round cuffs of facing colours. They had short skirts, turned back on the front edges to show the coarse white flannel linings. They were made with false pockets, straight across for battalion companies and slanting for flank and Highland companies. The coats were made of a very coarse, dirty brick-red, although the actual colour would vary considerably because of the poor dye and cloth quality.

*The 1796-pattern foot officer's sword, with its original scarlet and gold sword-knot and a Royal Artillery private's sword.* (Author's collection)

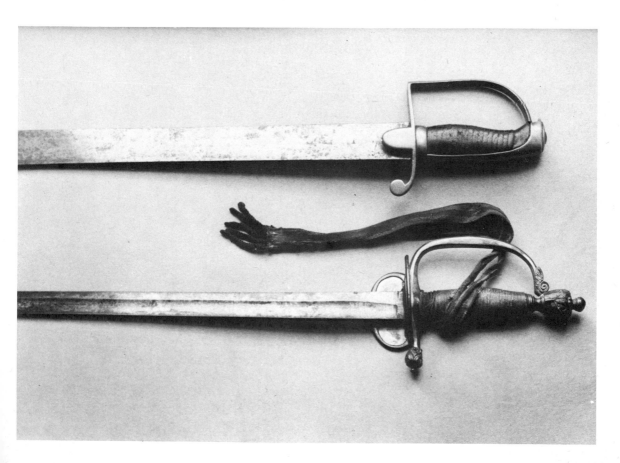

Regimental lace of wool worsted tape with different colours woven in it, as in the past, was sewn around the collar and shoulder-tabs, in bars across the breasts around the buttonholes, and on the cuffs and pocket buttonholes. Regiments with bastion lace had eight buttons on their coat-fronts, while those with rectangular lace had ten. The lace was really rather skimpy and coarse, the hand-sewing making it look as if it were actually drawn with a shaky hand. A triangle of lace was sewn between the two waist-level buttons on the back of the coat rear.

*This private of the 8th (King's) Regiment of Foot wears regimental lace with a yellow and a blue stripe. The uniform is virtually identical to all the regular regiments stationed in Canada at the war's beginning. (Youens/Osprey)*

*As an officer in the 43rd Regiment of Foot, one of the Light Division regiments, this lieutenant wears wings on both shoulders with bugle horns on each one. His regiment continued to wear the stovepipe shako after the Belgic was ordered, with green cords and tassels. (Youens/Osprey)*

Shoulder-tabs were pointed, square, or three-sided. At the end of each was a tuft or wing of hard, coarse, wool fringe.

Some coats were actually not even buttoned across the front, but simply fastened by hooks and eyes and made with false buttonholes and buttons.

Officers continued to have facing colour lapels, which they showed by unbuttoning a few of the top buttons and folding their coat open. For dress they buttoned all the lapels back and hooked the fronts together. While the men's coat-skirts were made shorter, the officers kept long skirts.

Breeches were still white, but gaiters were now made of black wool instead of linen, and reached to where the breeches ended at the knee. Men sent to America were issued with trousers to wear over their breeches, 'for the Sake of preserving them'.

Accoutrements and weapons were changed immediately after the last war, reflecting its lessons. Grenadiers were no longer to carry swords or match-cases. Light infantrymen were to be supplied with small priming horns, holding some two ounces of powder. Officers' spontoons, it was ordered on 29 April 1786,

'shall be laid aside, and that, in Lieu thereof, the Battalion Officers are, for the future, to make use of Swords. The Officers of all Infantry Corps shall be provided with a strong substantial Uniform Sword, the Blade of which is to be straight, and made to cut and thrust; to be One Inch at least broad at the Shoulder; and 32 Inches in Length. The Hilt if not of Steel, is to be either Gilt or Silver, according to the Colour of the Buttons on the Uniforms; and the Sword Knot, to be Crimson and Gold in Stripes, as required by the present Regulation.'

Grenadier, light infantry and fusilier officers were no longer to carry fusils. While officers lost their pole-arms, according to orders of 4 April 1792, 'The Serjeants of Infantry are to be supplied with, and to make use of Pikes, instead of the Halberds at present in use, which are to be laid aside.' It was later ordered that 'the Serjeants of Grenadiers, and Fuzileers, to carry Pikes: but the Light Infantry Serjeants are to keep their Fuzils, as at present'. This system of armament continued through 1815.

The tin waterbottle had been abandoned in favour of a wooden one, like the American canteen. It was painted a pale grey-blue, often with some sort

*The 104th Regiment of Foot's bayonet belt-plate.* (Rebecca Katcher)

of company or regimental number painted on one side, and hung by a leather strap from the right shoulder to the left side. The wooden waterbottle, although it will rot out eventually, will not rust like the tin variety.

The cartridge-box, which had grown to hold thirty-six rounds in the last war, was again increased to hold a staggering sixty rounds of ammunition. As eight rounds weighed about a pound, the box's weight may well be imagined. The box was still carried on a whitened buff leather sling with two buckles near the box to adjust the sling's length.

The trend begun in the last war of wearing the bayonet-belt across the shoulder instead of round the waist was now official. Virtually every regiment now wore white crossbelts with a rectangular plate on the bayonet-belt in the centre of the chest. These plates were engraved or cast with regimental badges, numbers, or whatever the colonel pleased.

The haversack was similar to that worn in the last war, although now closed with two buttons instead of three. The haversack, the waterbottle, the cartridge-box, and the bayonet-belt made up quite a number of belts to be hung from one's shoulders and, since there was no waistbelt to put over them and keep them from flapping about in action, the musket-sling was often taken from its hooks and buckled around the waist over the shoulder-belts. This, of course, was a non-regulation habit, but in the

Canadian wilderness, where units were apt to be small ones, such non-regulation practices were quite common.

By the War of 1812 the same general type of knapsack as had been used late in the last war was in use. By 1815 a black oilcloth knapsack, with whitened leather straps and breast harness and a regimental number or badge painted on its back, was adopted. Few, if any, of the 1815 period kit items ever reached the American battlefront.

While all accoutrements might not reach America promptly, orders did. One important set of orders changed the system of distinguishing rank. Privates still had plain uniforms. A new rank, that of 'Chosen Man', was added, and he had a single chevron of regimental lace on the upper arm, point down. The corporal had two similar chevrons. Sergeants still wore plain, not regimental, lace, and they had three plain white wool worsted chevrons. The regimental sergeant-major had four chevrons, but his were usually silver lace.

Another new rank was that of colour-sergeant, who now carried the regimental colours. No longer could the ensign be called the 'rag-carrier' as he had been in the late eighteenth century. The colour-sergeant wore a chevron of plain white lace on the upper right arm with a Union flag embroidered in full colour above it. There were also two crossed silver swords over the flag's staff and a crown embroidered in full colour.

In the flank companies, sergeants and company-sergeants-major wore chevrons on both arms. So did all the sergeants in light infantry regiments. Flank company colour-sergeants wore their special badge on their right arm and three chevrons on the left.

All chevrons were sewn to pieces of facing colour wool. Some regiments may have worn their chevron points up as well.

Officers also had their system of rank identification changed. The idea of simply having a single epaulette on the right shoulder and thus being able to know every officer in the Army wouldn't work in such an enlarged, far-flung army. Officers of the 93rd, a Highland regiment at New Orleans, wore two epaulettes. Companies of the light infantry regiments which served in America, the 43rd, 60th, and 95th, wore a wing on each shoulder with a grenade or bugle on the strap, as did flank company officers in regular regiments – the grenades being worn by grenadier company officers, the bugles by those of a light company.

Battalion company officers wore one epaulette on the right shoulder. The major had two, each with a star on it. The lieutenant-colonel's epaulettes had crowns on them, and the colonel's had both a crown and a star. Adjutants and quartermasters were to wear the same epaulettes or wings as the subalterns, although the adjutant also had a strap on his left shoulder. Paymasters, surgeons, and assistant surgeons were to wear no epaulettes, wings, nor even the crimson silk sashes which all the other officers wore.

Another major clothing change was to give the men an undress uniform. When not on duty they

*The coat worn by General Sir Isaac Brock at the battle of Queenston Heights. The arrow points to the fatal bullet-hole.* (Canadian War Museum)

*Other ranks' pewter buttons of, from left, the 8th (King's) Regiment of Foot, 10th Royal Veteran Battalion, 21st, 102nd, and 104th Regiments of Foot. (Rebecca Katcher)*

could wear plain coarse wool jackets, with cuffs, collars and shoulder-tabs of the facing colour. These were virtually identical to the red coats, only without lace or tails. In addition, a small wool cap, like those worn by Germans in the First World War, was authorized. A pompon of coarse woollen fringe was often worn on the top, rather like the tourie on the Highlander's bonnet.

Breeches in the infantry had been done away with early in America. They were originally replaced with white linen duck trousers, but by the time war broke out they were being made of grey wool. They were often locally made and therefore varied considerably from place to place. Dark grey wool gaiters were worn over the shoes, but under the trousers.

Boots, or shoes, varied, too. Articles called 'beef boots', which appear to have been ankle-length boots, were issued in Canada. A private of the 95th, shortly before his regiment was sent to New Orleans, wrote:

'I got a pair of boots, put them on, and threw my old ones away; but before I had walked four miles my other boot bottom dropped off, and I had to walk barefooted, as my stocking feet were soon cut all to pieces. I was not alone in this predicament; many of the men were served the same. These boots were manufactured in England, and we said the soles and heels had been glued or pegged on, as there could not have been any . . . hemp used. I had worn out my shirts; the one I had on did not reach to my waist. I found a sheet in a house from which its occupants had fled; and a tailor in the regiment had cut me a shirt out of it; so here I resolved to finish it if possible. I did it, and put it on.'

Troops in America were often in rags, with the difficulties in transporting equipment many miles first of ocean and then of wilderness. At least, the 95th was used to rags. Shortly before being sent to America another of their riflemen recalled how, 'there was scarcely a vestige of uniform among the men. Some of them were dressed in Frenchman's coats, some in white breeches and huge jack-boots, some with cocked hats and queues, most of their swords were fixed on their rifles, and stuck full of hams, tongues, and loaves of bread, and not a few were carrying bird-cages. There never was a better masked corps.'

That a regiment like the 95th might fall on such days is even more unbelievable when one realizes that their uniform was quite different from that worn by the rest of the Army and one in which the men took special pride.

The coat and trousers were dark green, since known as 'rifle green', cut basically the same as the rest of the Army. Collar and cuffs were black, and a black twisted cord was worn down the seam of each leg. Both collar and cuffs were edged with white. Instead of a single row of buttons, three rows of twelve black buttons were worn on the coat's front. Trousers were quite close-fitting, but loose-fitting ones were issued for guard, fatigue duties, and campaigning, and were probably worn at New Orleans.

The stovepipe shako was worn, with white cockades for the battalion except for those who were able to place four out of six shots on a target and rated as marksmen. They wore green cockades. The woollen plume for all was green, and a brass bugle horn was also worn on the shako.

The regiment was supplied with Baker rifles. They were 0·625 calibre – a considerably larger calibre than the American rifle – with a browned barrel and seven-groove rifling. A brass patch-box and brass fittings were used, and a long, brass-hilted sword-bayonet instead of the Bess's triangular bayonet. Barrels were about thirty inches long.

While an accurate weapon in the hands of a well-trained man, and superior to the Brown Bess, the Baker rifle suffered in comparison with the issue American rifle. Its heavier ball, fired through a shorter barrel, had much less of a range than the

American rifle. And, of course, the British rifleman had to carry a heavier load of ammunition than his American counterpart.

The other rifle regiment which served in America was the 60th. Its 5th and 6th Battalions were rifle units, the first in the British Army. According to the regulations of the 5th Battalion:

*Dress of the Royal Regiment of Artillery was unaffected by changes in infantry uniforms of the period, and it included breeches, leggings, and the stovepipe shako throughout the period.* (Youens/Osprey)

'The jackets of the private men of this battalion are of green cloth without lapels or lining and the jacket fronts faced with green cloth and made to button over the body down to the waist with nine buttons. The skirts rather short and lined green serge. The hind skirts fold over between the hip buttons and also turned back to the front skirts with a button in the joining and each have a slip of red cloth along the edges of the skirt lining, six darts of lace on each wing with which a red standing collar are laced round. The cuffs red cloth made pointed and to open at the wrist with two buttons. Shoulder straps of green cloth with red "feathered" edge. No pocket flaps and the pockets to open at the plait. The lace a scarlet worsted binding. A white milled serge waistcoat and blue cloth pantaloons. The rifle companies of the 1st, 2nd, 3rd, 4th, and 6th battalions of the 60th. Jackets for the rifle corps of the above are of green cloth, without lapels or lining. The inside of the breast fronts (faced) with red cloth and made

*A contemporary print of Royal Artillerymen.* (Parker Gallery)

to button over the body down to the waist with ten buttons. Short skirts not turned back but cut to slope behind with the pocket flaps sloping like Light Infantry and the pockets in the plait. Round cuffs with four buttons on each and without slits. The cuffs, shoulder straps and standing collar of green cloth. No wings or lace but the edges of the whole jacket feathered with red cloth. The back skirts to fold well over behind the hip button. All buttons of jacket white metal. White milled serge waistcoat with sleeves, green cloth breeches and black cloth woolen gaiters.'

*On duty, officers and men of the Royal Marines were allowed dark blue coatees with red collar, cuffs, and shoulder-tabs, with grey trousers – a sensible uniform for firing cannon. For dress, however, this captain wears the ordered scarlet coat and white breeches. His sword is the Army, not Navy, pattern.* (Youens/Osprey)

*Of all the regiments at New Orleans, the two West Indies Regiments probably suffered most from the cold, rainy weather. This private of the 5th West Indies Regiment had previously spent his life in tropical or semi-tropical weather – the same kind of weather the planners in London thought prevailed at New Orleans in January.* (Youens/Osprey)

Besides the rifle and musket, the other major weapon used in the War of 1812 was artillery. Artillery under Captain Jackson took part in the battle of Chrysler's Farm and later, on the retreat, at Fort Niagara. The Royal Regiment of Artillery had been unaffected by orders putting soldiers in pantaloons or the 1812 'Belgic' shako. They wore the stovepipe shako, with a special badge, throughout the period. Their coats were made like those of the rest of the Army, still with blue bodies, red facings, and yellow lace. Lace was worn in bastions. The knee-length gaiters and white pantaloons were used.

A new artillery weapon in America was the Congreve rocket. This was nothing more than a tube of gunpowder, fired from a smooth-bore barrel. Screaming and flitting from place to place with absolutely no accuracy or forewarning of where they would end up, these rockets were much more of a psychological weapon than a dangerous one.

In America they were generally handled by units of the Royal Marine Artillery, who were dressed like the Royal Regiment of Artillery, although the troops in America were supplied before they left with '4 blue jackets for sergeants; 4 blue jackets for drummers; 36 blue jackets for gunners; 36 pair of half-gaiters; 4 caps for sergeants; 76 caps for gunners; 80 knapsacks; 120 pairs grey trousers'.

At New Orleans, however, the men manning the Congreve rockets were members of the Rocket Brigade, Royal Horse Artillery. They were dressed like dragoons in leather helmets with enormous bearskin crests, short blue jackets, and fitted white breeches and black boots.

Another unusual set of units at New Orleans was the 1st and 5th West India Regiments. These were made up of black natives from the West Indies and sent to New Orleans under the thought that that southern port had a tropical climate all year around. It was actually quite a cold rainy January, and the units suffered as much or more from sickness than from American gunfire.

The two regiments wore uniforms similar to the rest of the infantry, with some changes to suit the tropics. The coats were made with half-lapels and no skirts. Sleeves were unlined. While shoulder-straps, lapels, and cuffs were white for the 1st Regiment and green for the 5th, all collars were red. The men wore Russian duck gaitered trousers. Light

*Top, the stovepipe shako-plate, and the 'Belgic' shako-plate, bottom.* (Rebecca Katcher)

leather slippers were issued rather than heavy infantry boots to these men who had gone barefoot all their lives. Probably in America most of the men wore the stovepipe shakos, although some of the newly designed shakos might have been issued by them.

The new shako had been ordered for the whole

Army in 1812, although it is doubtful if many reached America during the war. It had a simpler brass plate, and the tuft on the side, while white cords came from each side to meet in the middle. A foul-weather, black oilcloth cover was issued and probably widely used. Light infantrymen continued to wear the old stovepipes.

Another regiment which did not use the new 'Belgic' shako was the 93rd, the Sutherland High-landers, which arrived in America in time for the battle of New Orleans. The 93rd wore the standard Highland regiments' fatigue cap, the Hummell bonnet, which had a tall band of red and white dicing with a small dark blue crown topped by a tourie. The tourie was red for battalion companies, white for grenadiers, and green for the light com-pany. Officers wore a silver badge with a spray of two thistles and the number 93 in the centre of their bonnets.

The 93rd, the only Highland regiment to serve in America during the War of 1812, did not wear kilts. Thinking the campaign in America would be fought in rougher country than Europe, their govern-ment set kilts had been converted into trews.

Other than that, their kit was virtually identical to every other regiment in the Army, and they carried the same load of musket, cartridge-box, haversack, waterbottle, and the rest. An officer of the 84th Regiment of Foot, reporting on the Army's movement towards Washington in 1814, wrote that 'The load which they carried . . . was far from trifling. (Probably thirty pounds at least.) Inde-

*From left, an officer's cap-badges and a sword-belt plate of the 93rd (Sutherland Highlanders) Regiment of Foot.*

pendent of their arms and sixty rounds of ball cartridge, each man bore upon his back a knapsack containing shirts, stockings, etc., a blanket, a haver-sack with provisions for three days, and a canteen or wooden keg filled with water.'

This load, the problem of resupplying units in the wilderness, and, it must be admitted, a greater interest in fighting abilities than dress among many officers, meant that the troops in America wore considerably less uniform than some people would have liked them to have had. Said one of the Duke of Wellington's officers: 'provided we brought our men into the field well appointed, and with sixty rounds of good ammunition each, he never looked to see whether their trowsers were black, blue or grey, and as to ourselves [the officers] we might be rigged out in all colours of the rainbow if we fancied it'.

This did not go well in Canada where General Sir George Prevost, no Iron Duke, was in charge. On 23 August 1814 he issued the following order:

'The Commander of the Forces has observed in the dress of Several of the Officers of Corps & Departments, lately added to this Army from that of Field Marshal the Duke of Wellington, a fancible vanity inconsistent with the rules of the Service, and in Some instances without Comfort or Convenience and to the prejudice of the Service, by removing essential distinctions of Rank and description of Service.

'His Excellency deems it expedient to direct that the General Officers in Charge of Divisions & Brigades do uphold His Majesty's Commands in that respect, and only admit of such deviations from them as may be justified by particular causes of

Service and Climate – and even then uniformity is to be retained.

'Commanding Officers are held responsible that the Established Uniform of their Corps is strictly observed by the Officers under their Command.'

Such an order did not endear Prevost to the hard-

The only Highland Regiment to serve in America during the War of 1812 was the 93rd. Its kilts were made into trews before it left England. Sergeants and officers wore their sashes across their bodies, and sergeants carried pikes instead of muskets in the grenadier and battalion companies. (Roffe/Osprey)

A fully equipped private of the 93rd (Sutherland Highlanders), which was the regiment to take the largest beating at New Orleans. The regiment was drawn up under American fire where it simply stood silently, without orders, taking fantastic losses.

bitten veterans of the Peninsular campaign, who had really been looking for a spot of rest at home rather than another war in the colonies.

He could, on the other hand, get away with that with the militia under his command. His militia from Lower Canada, the largest of the two Canadian colonies and made up mostly of Frenchmen, had some 60,000 men, described as 'a mere posse, ill arm'd, and without discipline'. To improve matters, 2,000 bachelors between the ages of eighteen and twenty-five were drafted for service of between three months to a year in four select embodied militia battalions. A fifth, known as the 'Devil's Regiment' because of the 'thieving and disorderly propensities' of its men, was raised later. It was later reorganized as the Canadian Chasseurs in March 1814, and given green coats with black facings.

A 6th Battalion was raised for garrison duties in Quebec and two temporary militia light infantry battalions were used during the 1813 summer campaign, and then returned to their own battalions.

The men were first supplied with 'red cloth . . . brown linen for lining . . . trousers . . . buttons . . . hats or caps . . . cockades . . . privates loopings'. Haversacks, fifes and drums, and sergeants' pikes were also issued. Officers wore red coats with white facings and thin gold lace edging the collar and cuffs, but they had no epaulettes or sashes.

While officers may have had red coats, red cloth for the men's coats was harder to obtain. As a result, coats were mostly made of green. The 1st Battalion managed to find enough red wool for most of their men and were even 'in hopes of being able to procure some surplus jackets of the King's Regiment' by March 1813. In that year the 1st Battalion, probably taking their cue from the blue facings of the King's, was assigned blue facings. The 2nd had light green; the 3rd yellow; the 4th dark green; and the 5th and 6th black. They all also received stores consisting of 'Caps & plumes, Red Coats, Waistcoats with sleeves, Blue Trowsers, Forage Caps, Gaiters, Linen Shirts, Shoes, Knapsacks' and 'Stocks and Clasps'.

Upper Canada (Ontario today) was founded by men of the last war's provincial corps. A much smaller province than Lower Canada, its militia officers were to wear scarlet coats faced blue with plain gilt buttons. As of March 1812, each militia regiment was to have two flank companies, which

received more training and were the first to be called up when war began.

They, too, suffered from the lack of supplies of uniforms in the colony. At first the militia was to come out in 'a short coat of some dark coloured cloth made to button well round the body, and pantaloons suited to the season, with the addition of a

*In terms of lace or bright facings this corporal of the 95th has a much duller uniform than the rest of the Army. It was, however, highly functional for the scouting and rough duties the regiment performed.* (Youens/Osprey)

round hat.' Officers were 'to dress in conformity with the men, in order to avoid the bad consequences of a conspicious dress.' Later, enough material was sent to make red coats with yellow facings, along with shakos, bicorn hats and 130 'leather light infantry caps'.

The men also wore spare red-faced uniforms of the 41st Regiment of Foot. This odd mixture of clothing lasted throughout the war. In January 1813 they were to wear 'green jackets, red cuff and collar and white lace; blue gunmouth trousers, and a felt regulation cap'. The next year they received green coats faced yellow and red coats with light and dark green facings, along with the necessary trousers,

shoes, and other uniform items.

Officers, by a militia general order of 21 June 1814, were to,

'appear in a scarlet jacket with dark blue facings, yellow buttons, gold lace round the Collar and Cuffs only, and plain gold epaulettes according to their rank. Grey Pantaloons or Trowsers & Cap according to His Majesty's Regulations for Regiments of the Line, but where such cannot be provided Round Hats will be permitted with a Regulation Feather, Cockade on the left side – The jacket to be made according to the King's order for Corps of the Line. . . . The Uniform of General Staff

144

Officers and Departments is to be similar to that of the . . . Regular Forces.'

Regardless of orders, a British officer later wrote that 'some had red coats and blue or red facings, some had green coats, but most had no coats at all'.

Besides the militia, there was once again a provincial corps which served full time and was liable to be sent anywhere required. A battalion, the Volunteer Incorporated Militia, was raised in early 1813 and issued with red coats with dark green facings, although next year these were changed to blue facings.

An Incorporated Artillery Company, raised in 1813, had the same dress as the Royal Artillery, while a Corps of Provisional Artillery Drivers received blue jackets with red cuffs and collars.

Out along the western Canadian frontiers the old standby, rangers, was raised. The Western Rangers, also called Caldwell's Rangers, served with the

*Contemporary painting of Sir Isaac Brock* (Public Archives of Canada)

Indians, wearing dark plain green jackets, grey trousers, and 'a low bucket cap, quite plain'. The Niagara Frontier Guides, originally called the Troop of Provincial Light Dragoons, wore blue jackets with red facings, felt helmets with bearskin decorations. and grey overalls wrapped with leather. Their footwear was 'Canadian beef half boots to lace in front'.

*The 1st Battalion of Select Embodied Militia's bayonet belt-plate.* (Rebecca Katcher)

*In the field, British general officers, like this major-general, wore an undecorated scarlet coat. The major-general's coat has its buttons in pairs.* (Youens/Osprey)

Probably the most famous of the provincial regiments were the Glengarry Light Infantry and the Canadian Voltigeurs. The Glengarries were originally raised as a Highland regiment to have full Highland dress, but quickly changed to a uniform 'to be green, like that of the 95th Rifles'. Its officers probably still clung to Highland weapons, however, carrying broadswords and dirks instead of the typical curved light infantry officer's sword.

The Canadian Voltigeurs were originally raised to carry 'rifles or light infantry muskets with black accoutrements: the clothing to be grey with black collars and cuffs and black buttons with Canadian short boots. Light Bear Skin caps.' The officers, however, wore rifle-green uniforms, while the men did actually receive grey ones. The visored bearskin caps were later replaced by regular light infantry shakos.

In many ways provincial officers may have been better than their British superiors, at least until the Peninsular campaign veterans arrived in 1814. A Canadian wrote that 'we got the rubbish of every department in the army. Any man whom the Duke deemed unfit for the Peninsula was considered quite good enough for the Canadian market.' General Isaac Brock called the 41st Regiment of Foot 'wretchedly officered'.

In addition, the regiments which had been stationed in Canada before the war were scattered in small posts throughout the country, making discipline difficult if not impossible. Men saw how quite poor men were becoming great property-owners and, if not men of wealth, at least of greater position in society than they would have had in 'the old country'. The country swarmed with American agents, talking the men into desertion. Desertion in large numbers became common.

Brock felt the answer to the problems in Canada

*King's Colour of the Quebec Militia.* (Canadian War Museum)

would be the posting of a Royal Veteran Battalion to the colony, which was done in 1808. Such a battalion was made up of 'Meritorious Soldiers, who by Wounds, Infirmity, or Age, are become unequal to the more active Duties of the Line, but who retain sufficient Strength for the less Laborious Duties of a Garrison . . .'. The Battalion raised for this duty was the 10th, and each man was awarded 200 acres of land for enlisting in it.

With the land to work, the men may have been more settled, but they shared the regulars' faults. One commander of a company of them said they were 'so debilitated and worn down by unconquerable drunkenness that neither the fear of punishment, the love of fame nor the honour of country can animate them to extraordinary exertions'.

It may have been difficult to animate the worn out soldiers of the 10th Royal Veteran Battalion, but the rest of the Army was inspired by years of magnificent performances, and was thoroughly professional. Their operations were carried out smoothly, with that well-oiled movement one could expect of regulars.

*The vast majority of men of the 1st Battalion of Lower Canadian Embodied Militia seem to have managed to find red coats, although many more may have worn green coats as did the other five battalions. The militia never received the new-issue shakos or, in fact, even their ordered colours until some years after the war.* (Youens/Osprey)

The operation on Washington was typical of how professionals in action could manœuvre. Wrote an officer on the expedition:

'Each boatload of soldiers . . . drew up the moment they stepped on shore, forming line without regard to companies or battalions; whilst parties were instantly dispatched to reconnoiter, and to take possession of every house, as well as to line every hedge in front of the shore where their comrades were arriving.

'So much time was unavoidably expended in establishing the different regiments on the ground allotted to them, in bringing up the hospital and commissariat stores, and arranging the material that, when all things were ready, the day appeared too far spent to permit an advance into a country the nature and military situation of which we were of course ignorant. The afternoon was accordingly devoted into a proper distribution of the force; which was divided into three brigades, in the following order.

'The first, or light brigade, consisted of the Eighty-fifth, the light infantry companies of the Fourth, Twenty-first and Forty-fourth Regiments, with the party of disciplined Negroes and a company of Marines, amounting in all to about 1,100 men; to the command of which Colonel William Thornton of the Eighty-fifth Regiment was appointed.

'The second brigade, composed of the Fourth (King's Own) and Forty-fourth Regiments, which mustered together 1,460 bayonets, was entrusted to the care of Colonel Arthur Brooke of the Forty-fourth.

'The third, made up of the Twenty-first and the battalion of marines and equalling the number of the second brigade was commanded by Colonel William Patterson of the Twenty-first.

'The whole of the infantry may therefore be estimated at 4,020 men.

'Besides these, there were landed about 100 artillerymen and an equal number of drivers; but for the want of horses to drag them, no more than one 6-pounder and two small 3-pounder guns were brought on shore. Except those belonging to the general and staff officers, there was not a single horse in the whole army. To have taken on shore a large park of artillery would have been, under the circumstances, absolute folly; indeed the pieces which were actually landed proved in the end of very little service, and were drawn by seamen sent from the different ships for the purpose.

*Battalion Colour of the Quebec Militia.* (Canadian War Museum)

'The sailors thus employed may be rated at 100, and those occupied in carrying stores, ammunition and other necessaries at 100 or more. Thus, by adding these together with 50 sappers and miners to the above amount, the whole number of men landed at St. Benedict's may be computed at 4,500.'

The small, highly professional army then encamped on the back slope of a hill near the shore so that the Americans could not make out their numbers or distributions if they were to attack. An advanced picket line was sent out around the camp.

The next day the men marched on towards where the Americans were waiting.

'The advanced guard, consisting of three companies of infantry, led the way. These, however, were preceded by a section of twenty men moving before them at the distance of 100 yards; and even these twenty were but the followers of two files sent forward to prevent suprise and to give warning of the approach of the enemy.

'Parallel with the head of the three companies, marched the flank patrols; parties of forty or fifty men which, extending in files from each side of the road, swept the woods and fields to the distance of nearly half a mile.

'After the advanced guard, leaving an interval of 100 or 150 yards came the light brigade, which, as well as the advance, sent out flankers to secure itself against ambuscades. Next to it, again, marched the second brigade, moving steadily on, leaving the skirmishing and reconnoitering to those in front. Then came the artillery . . . and last of all came the third brigade, leaving a detachment at the same distance from the rear of the column as the advanced guard was from its front.'

It was the policy that, when moving through enemy territory, the Army would march from defensible position to defensible position. If this was only eight or ten miles, then they would halt after marching only eight or ten miles. If there were no positions which appeared on the march, they could go twenty-five miles or more before quitting for the day. On the first day's march to Washington, it was 'upon this principle [the day's march was] extremely short, the troops halting when they had arrived at a rising ground distant not more than six miles from the point whence they set out. Having stationed the pickets, planted the sentinels, and made such other arrangements as the case required, fires were lighted and the men were suffered to lie down.'

It was in action, as well as in marching and landing, that the true professionalism of the British soldier was shown. In Europe the French had attacked in massed columns and the British answer had been to abandon the old practice of firing from three-deep ranks. It had been noted that the third rank either failed to fire at all, or they fired so high that their bullets went totally over their enemy's heads. The Army then switched to a system of firing in two ranks.

Old habits die hard sometimes. An American eyewitness at the night fight before the battle of New Orleans noted that the British 'still kept up the old custom of firing three deep; one row of men half-kneeling, and the other two ranks firing over their shoulders. This style of firing, along with the darkness of the evening, explained to me the reason of why the enemy's balls, which we heard whistling by, mostly flew over our heads.'

More than just abilities and discipline were usually needed on the early American battlefields. Martial music, played by fifes and drums, was a great builder of morale.

British musicians at first wore the reverse of their regimental colours. In a green-faced regiment, the musicians would wear green coats with red facings,

*The Glengarry Light Infantry had both brass and pewter bayonet belt-plates.* (Rebecca Katcher)

The uniform of the Glengarry Light Infantry Fencibles, raised in Canada, was copied from that of the 95th. The regiment was made up of Scotsmen, and many of its officers carried dirks and broadswords instead of the standard light infantry officer's accoutrements. (Youens/Osprey)

Officers like this captain of the Canadian Voltigeurs wore green uniforms, although their men wore grey faced black. The light infantry shako was issued in 1814, and before then both officers and men wore small bearskin caps with visors. (Youens/Osprey)

The perfectly regulation uniform, including the Belgic shako, is worn by this private of the 7th (Royal Fusiliers) Regiment of Foot in 1815 during the New Orleans campaign. For dress, officers and men wore bearskin caps, and in foul weather an oil-cloth over their felt shakos. (Youens/Osprey)

In the field in Canada sergeants, like this one of the 10th Royal Veteran Battalion, probably set aside their pikes in favour of muskets and cartridge-boxes. The battalion had been issued old-style white breeches and black gaiters and was allowed to wear them out before changing into grey trousers. (Youens/Osprey)

and so forth. In addition, their sleeves were often decorated with chevrons of regimental lace and they wore laced wings and bearskin caps with distinctive cap-plates like those of earlier grenadiers.

Unfortunately, this uniform stood out much too well in action. Therefore, the following order was issued on 25 September 1811:

'That the consequence of the nature of the duties to which Trumpeters and Buglers are unavoidably exposed on service and in consequence attending their loss in action, which is ascribed to the marked difference of their dress, their clothing may be of the same colour as that worn by their respective regiments and that the distinction which it is necessary to preserve between them and the privates may be pointed out by the lace.'

Musicians in Royal regiments had always worn the regular red coats with blue facings. At the same time, musicians wore the same shako as the rest of the Army instead of their old unique caps.

In this day, when we automatically associate pipers with Highland regiments, it is strange to think that few pipers at all were in the Highland regiments during the early American wars. Pipers were not allowed by regulation, and such as the regiments had were either civilians hired by the officers or carried on the rolls as drummers or privates. It was not until February 1854 that pipers were allowed in Highland regiments and only two years earlier the 91st and 92nd Regiments were ordered to be rid of theirs, as they were 'without authority'.

There were, nonetheless pipers in the regiments. In 1768 the 42nd had six fifers, and two pipers, who were listed as drummers. They still had two pipers in 1773.

Pipes carried the government sett tartan; and the 93rd at New Orleans had yellow drone ribbons on their pipes, save those of the light company piper who had green and yellow.

Fifes, the more common instruments, were made of wood and two were issued to each fifer, one for the tune and one for harmony. They were carried in an oval brass fife-case which had the regimental badge or number engraved or stamped on the front. The fife-case was suspended on red and facing colour strings attached to a wide whitened buff leather belt.

Early drums were painted with red hoops, although different-coloured hoops appeared by 1812. Those of the 93rd, for example, probably had yellow and red diagonal lines. Drum-fronts throughout the period were painted the facing colour, with a plain GR and crown and the regimental number, or the unit's particular badge.

There had been changes in every aspect of the music and, indeed, in all the rest of the British Army since it had become involved in its first major war in America, and there had been just as many changes in the American and French armies. And, with the signing of the Treaty of Ghent in 1814, and the final battle at Waterloo, never again would Briton, American, and Frenchman face each other on the field of battle. May it always be so.

# Select Bibliography

Alberts, Robert C., *The Most Extraordinary Adventures of Major Robert Stobo*, Boston, 1956.

Berg, Fred Anderson, *Encyclopedia of Continental Army Units*, Harrisburg, 1972.

Carman, W. Y., *The Royal Artillery*, Reading, 1973.

Cuthbertson, Captain, *System for the Interior Management and Oeconomy of an Infantry Battalion*, London, 1768.

Darling, Anthony, *Red Coat and Brown Bess*, Ottawa, 1968.

Eelking, Max von, *The German Allied Troops in the North American War of Independence*, translated by J. G. Rosengarten, Albany, New York, 1893.

Fortesque, J. W., *A History of the British Army*, London; various volumes, various dates.

Hamilton, Edward P., *The French Army in America*, Ottawa, 1967.

Jacobs, James Ripley, *The Beginning of The U.S. Army*, Princeton, New Jersey, 1947.

*Journal of the Society for Army Historical Research*, London; various issues.

Katcher, Philip, *King George's Army, 1775–1783*, Reading, 1973; Harrisburg, Pennsylvania, 1973.

Kreidbert, Lieutenant-Colonel M. A., and Henry, Lieutenant M. G., *History of Military Mobilization in the United States Army 1775–1945*, Washington, D.C., 1955.

Lawson, C. C. P., *A History of Uniforms of the British Army*, London, various volumes, various dates.

Lefferts, Charles, *A History of Uniforms of the American, British, French and Germans in the War of the American Revolution, 1775–1783*, New York, 1926.

Lewis, Berkeley, R., *Small Arms and Ammunition in the United States Service, 1776–1865*, Baltimore, 1956.

*Military Collector & Historian*, Washington, D.C.; various issues.

Nesmith, James H., *The Soldier's Manual*, Philadelphia, 1824.

Peterson, Harold L., *Arms and Armor in Colonial America, 1526–1783*, Harrisburg, 1956.

Peterson, Harold L., *The Book of the Continental Soldier*, Harrisburg, 1968.

*Regulations and Orders for the* [British] *Army*, London, 1816.

*Rules and Regulations for the Army of the United States*, Cambridge, Mass., 1814.

Shields, Joseph W., Jnr, *From Flintlock to M1*, New York, 1954.

Simes, Thomas, *The Military Guide for Young Officers*, London, 1776.

Smith, Captain George, *An Universal Military Dictionary*, London, 1779.

*Standing Orders and Regulations for the Army in Ireland*, Dublin, 1794.

Steuben, Baron von, *Regulations for the Order and Discipline of the Troops of the United States*, Philadelphia, 1779.

de Watteville, Colonel H., *The British Soldier*, New York; no date given.

Windrow, Martin and Wilkinson, Frederick, eds., *The Universal Soldier*, Enfield, 1972.

Windrow, Martin, *Montcalm's Army*, Reading, 1973.

Wolfe, James, *Instructions to Young Officers*, London, 1780.

# Index